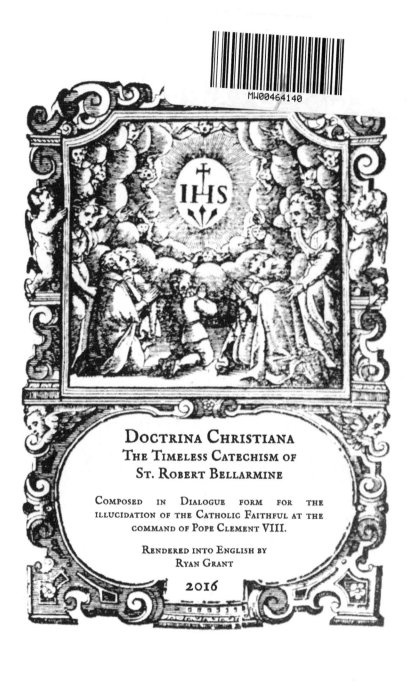

DOCTRINA CHRISTIANA
THE TIMELESS CATECHISM OF
ST. ROBERT BELLARMINE

COMPOSED IN DIALOGUE FORM FOR THE
ILLUCIDATION OF THE CATHOLIC FAITHFUL AT THE
COMMAND OF POPE CLEMENT VIII.

RENDERED INTO ENGLISH BY
RYAN GRANT

2016

DOCTRINA CHRISTIANA

THE TIMELESS CATECHISM OF
ST. ROBERT BELLARMINE
DOCTOR OF THE CHURCH;
PATRON OF CATECHISTS

TRANSLATED FROM THE LATIN BY
RYAN GRANT

WITH A NEW INTRODUCTION BY
HIS EXCELLENCY

BISHOP ATHANASIUS SCHNEIDER
AUXILIARY BISHOP OF OUR LADY OF ASTANA

MEDIATRIX PRESS
MMXVI
www.mediatrixpress.com

ISBN-10: 0692758909
ISBN-13: 978-0692758908

Translated From:
Doctrina Christiana
Catechismus, seu Explicatio Doctrinae Christianae
By St. Robert Bellarmine
Cardinal of the Society of Jesus
Bishop of Capua
Published at Prague, 1747

The Fell types are digitally reproduced by Igino Marini, www.iginomarini.com.
Used with permission.

TABLE OF CONTENTS

CHAPTER I

What Christian Doctrine is and what are its Principal Parts..................... 1

CHAPTER II

An Explanation of the Sign of the Holy Cross............................ 5

CHAPTER III

Explanation of the Creed, that is, of the Twelve Articles..................... 13

Explanation of the First Article................ 14
Explanation of the Second Article............ 18
Explanation of the Third Article.............. 21
Explanation of the Fourth Article............ 25
Explanation of the Fifth Article.............. 31
Explanation of the Sixth Article............. 36
Explanation of the Seventh Article.......... 40
Explanation of the Eighth Article........... 43
Explanation of the Ninth Article............ 46
Explanation of the Tenth Article............ 53
Explanation of the Eleventh Article......... 54
Explanation of the Twelfth Article.......... 57

CHAPTER IV

An Explanation of the OUR FATHER. . 63

CHAPTER V

An Explanation of the HAIL MARY. ... 85

CHAPTER VI

An Explanation of the Decalogue, or the Ten Commandments of GOD.......... 95

Explanation of the First Commandment..... 100

Explanation of the Second Commandment. . 110

Explanation of the Third Commandment.... 118

Explanation of the Fourth Commandment... 123

Explanation of the Fifth Commandment..... 126

Explanation of the Sixth Commandment. ... 129

Explanation of the Seventh Commandment.. 132

Explanation of the Eighth Commandment... 135

Explanation of the Ninth Commandment.... 139

Explanation of the Tenth Commandment... 141

CHAPTER VII

An Explanation of the Precepts of the Church. 145

CHAPTER VIII

An Explanation on Evangelical Counsels 147

CHAPTER IX

An Explanation of the Sacraments of the Holy Church.................... 151

On Baptism.......................... 156

On Confirmation. 161

On the Most Holy Eucharist.............. 163

On Penance........................... 174

On Extreme Unction. 181

On the Sacrament of Order.............. 183

On the Sacrament of Marriage........... 184

CHAPTER X
> *On the Virtues in General.* 187

CHAPTER XI
> *On the Theological Virtues in General*
> 191

CHAPTER XII
> *On the Cardinal Virtues.* 195

CHAPTER XIII
> *On the Seven Gifts of the Holy Spirit*
> 201

CHAPTER XIV
> *On the Eight Beatitudes.* 205

CHAPTER XV
> *On the Seven Corporal Works of Mercy*
> *and the Seven Spiritual Works of Mercy*
> 209

CHAPTER XVI
> *On Vices and Sins in General.* 214

CHAPTER XVII
> *On Original Sin.* 218

CHAPTER XVIII
> *On Mortal and Venial Sin..* 222

CHAPTER XIX
> *On the Seven Capital Sins.* 226

CHAPTER XX
   On Sins against the Holy Spirit...... 235

CHAPTER XXI
   On Sins Crying to Heaven for Vengeance
.... 239

CHAPTER XXII
   On the Four Last Things. 241

Introduction

"THERE is nothing more effective than catechetical instruction to spread the glory of God and to secure the salvation of souls" (Pope Benedict XIV, Apostolic Constitution, *Etsi minime*). Saint Pius X said, that the great loss of souls is due to ignorance of divine things (cf. Encyclical *Acerbo nimis*).

Our Lord Jesus Christ gave to His Apostles, and though them, to all holders of the Magisterium of the Church the solemn and weighty duty to teach the truths of the faith to all people of all times until He comes again (cf. Mt 28: 19). The believers in Christ have, as well, the duty to learn and to know the Divinely revealed truths. The bishops and their first collaborators the priests, especially the parish priests, must nourish the faithful with the Divine food of the truth and of the sacraments. They have to be "that faithful and wise steward, whom his Lord shall make ruler over his household, to give them their portion of meat in due season" (Lk 12: 42). The Council of Trent, treating of the duties of pastors of souls, decreed that their first and most important work is the instruction of the faithful (cf. *Sess.* V, cap. 2, *De*

Reform.; *Sess.* XXII, cap. 8; *Sess.* XXIV, cap. 4 & 7, *De Reform*).

Each faithful Catholic must be able to repeat with all his heart the words of Saint Paul: "I know Whom I have believed" (2 Tim 2: 12). A true Catholic has to know, therefore, his faith. An essential characteristic of a Catholic consists in keeping the truths of the faith faithfully and purely according to the Apostolic admonition: "Continue in the things which you have learned and have been assured of, knowing of whom you have learned them" (2 Tim 3: 14). Paraphrasing the words of Saint Paul in the Letter to the Romans 10: 14, one could say: How then shall the faithful know Christ when they have not been taught? And how shall they be taught without a good catechism?

In our time we are witnessing an unprecedented crisis of the faith inside the Church, which last already more than fifty years and which is marked by a widespread ignorance of the Catholic truths and at the same by a general confusion regarding their immutable validity. The following words of Saint Pius X, spoken over a hundred years ago, are highly up to date and fully applicable to our times: "We are forced to agree with those who hold that the chief cause of the present indifference and, as it were, infirmity of soul, and the serious evils that result from it, is to be found above all in ignorance of things divine. This is fully in accord with what God Himself declared through the Prophet Osee: "And there is no knowledge of God in the land." (Osee 4: 1). [...] The corruption of morals and depravity of life is already so great, and ever increasingly greater, not only among uncivilized peoples but even in those very nations that are called Christian. The Apostle Paul, writing to the Ephesians, repeatedly admonished them in these words: "But immorality and every uncleanness or covetousness, let it not even be named among you, as become saints; or obscenity or foolish talk" (Eph. 5:34). He also places the foundation of holiness and sound morals upon a knowledge of divine things—which holds in check evil desires: "See to it therefore, brethren, that you walk with care: not as unwise but as wise. . . Therefore, do not become foolish, but understand what the will of the Lord is" (Eph. 5:15-16)." (Encyclical *Acerbo nimis* from April 15, 1905).

A good and solid knowledge of the Catholic faith has as its aim a virtuous life through which alone with the help of God's grace one can achieve eternal salvation. Saint Pius X teaches therefore: "Christian teaching not only bestows on the intellect the light by which it attains truth, but from it our will draws that ardor by which we are raised up to God and joined with Him in the practice of virtue" (Encyclical *Acerbo nimis* from April 15, 1905).

The true knowledge of the Catholic faith fills the human mind with a light and this light, in spite of being sometimes obfuscated by a bad will, is usually the effective means of salvation. "A man who walks with open eyes may, indeed, turn aside from the right path, but a blind man is in much more imminent danger of wandering away. Furthermore, there is always some hope for a reform of perverse conduct so long as the light of faith is not entirely extinguished; but if lack of faith is added to depraved morality because of ignorance, the evil hardly admits of remedy, and the road to ruin lies open." (Encyclical *Acerbo nimis* from April 15, 1905).

Saint Pius X, the great catechist on the Papal throne, made the following luminous and at the same time highly realistic observation: "How many and how grave are the consequences of ignorance in matters of religion! And on the other hand, how necessary and how beneficial is religious instruction! It is indeed vain to expect a fulfillment of the duties of a Christian by one who does not even know them" (Encyclical *Acerbo nimis* from April 15, 1905).

INTRODUCTION

In our time of an enormous and general confusion in matters of Catholic faith we do need urgently a crystal-clear, absolute reliable and at the same time simple Catechetical text. Such a text represents the famous Catechism of Saint Robert Bellarmine, which notwithstanding being written four hundred years ago, remains nevertheless up to date. This catechism had until the 20th century about 400 editions and has been translated in 60 languages. It was a favorite catechetical tool for the missionaries in the past centuries.

The countries of the so-called Western civilization became today almost neo-pagan societies, and there are even people who name themselves Catholics but are living like pagans. It is therefore obvious that we are living in a missionary period both inside and outside the Church.

Mr. Ryan Grant, who operates Mediatrix Press, has the merit of publishing in our days the Catechism of Saint Robert Bellarmine in English. This catechism can be considered as a valid and effective catechetical tool for the work of the evangelization, a work which has to be realized with a new missionary zeal towards those who don't know the Catholic faith and as well towards those who know it defectively and insufficiently.

INTRODUCTION

May those who will read this catechism, as well as those who will use it in the noble and meritorious work of teaching Christian doctrine, may be equipped with the sure and sacred doctrine of the Catholic faith, in order to stand, having their loins girt about with truth, and having on the breastplate of righteousness; and their feet shod with the preparation of the gospel of peace; above all, they shall take the shield of faith, wherewith they shall be able to quench all the fiery darts of the wicked (cf. Eph 6: 14-16). In this way, they will be ready always to give an answer to every man that asks them the reason of their hope, with meekness and fear (cf. 1 Peter 3: 15-16).

The integral truth of the Catholic faith will set people free (cf. John 8: 32), because it is not a human, but a Divine truth. Indeed, each human person has been created in order "to know, serve and love God, to offer all of creation in this world in thanksgiving back to him and to be raised up to life with him in heaven" (*Compendium of the Catechism of the Catholic Church*, 67).

July 7, 2016

✠ ATHANASIUS SCHNEIDER
Auxiliary Bishop
of the Archdiocese of Saint Mary in Astana

xvi

ST. ROBERT BELLARMINE composed two catechisms under the title of *Doctrina Christiana* (Christian Doctrine), one called his "Small Catechism" which he had written for children and simple souls. This second one, written as a dialogue, called his "Long Catechism," was intended for teachers and for the well instructed to deepen their understanding of the truths of the faith. The Shorter Catechism was translated in 1614, but the Long, at least to our knowledge, had never been rendered into English until now.

The translation was made from the Latin edition published in Prague in 1732. It seemed to be the most accurate, and it was compiled and edited into a text version by Anton Repko, whom I especially thank as many of the copies available in electronic form have defects, missing pages etc. Still, as sometimes the Latin edition used complicated phrases from 16th century vernacular Latin that simply would not render into English well, it was necessary to consult Bellarmine's original Italian to simplify.

Additionally, we have added, in this edition, a number of woodcuts from the 1614 English translation of the Short Catechism, which we thought would be fitting for the first translation of the Long Catechism.

This Catechism was written at the express command of Pope Clement VIII, and approved by him in 1598. It quickly became more popular than the Saint's *Controversies*, which he is principally known for today. It was also specifically approved by Pope Benedict XIV, and its importance was so great that Pius XI, in his declaration making the saint a doctor of the Church, declared of this Catechism:

"Nor may we pass-over in silence his sacred sermons and also his catechetical works, especially that Catechism, which the use of the ages as well as the judgment of a great many Bishops and Doctors of the Church has approved. Indeed, in that same catechism, composed at the command of Clement VIII, the illustrious holy theologian expounded for the use of the Christian people and especially of children, the Catholic truth in a plain style, so brilliantly, exactly and orderly that for nearly three centuries in many regions of Europe and the world, it most fruitfully provided the fodder of Christian doctrine to the faithful."[1]

---

[1] «Nec silentio praetereunda sunt eius sacrae conciones atque opera catechetica vel praesertim Catechismus ille, quem saeculorum usus et plurimorum Episcoporum doctorumque Ecclesiae iudicium comparavit. Eodem

As his Excellency, Bishop Schneider, has noted in his introductory remarks, this Catechism remains up to date; nevertheless, there are a few places where the discipline of his time has been changed by the Church, and in those places I have left a footnote to indicate the current law.

I hope that this Catechism will be of profound benefit for Catechists whose mission it is to prepare the Christian faithful to live a full Christian life, having at their disposal a Catechism written by the Patron of Catechists especially for them.

Ryan Grant
Post Falls, ID
10 July, 2016

---

profecto Catechismo, Clementis Pp. VIII iussu composito, insignis sanctus theologus ad christianae plebis ac praesertim parvulorum usum catholicam veritatem plano stylo, ita nitide, exacte qtque ex ordine exposuit, ut tria fere per saecula in multis, Europae et orbis regionibus Christianae doctrinae pabulum fideli populo fructuosissime ipse praebuerit.» AAS 23 [1931] 436.

DEDICATIO

Uxori meae
plenitudini virtutum
magnopere longaminis humilitatisque quâ
victorias retulit, confrégit vitia
et adeo meruit quot coronas tot liberos dedit
ut comparate cum virtutibus suis
exigua sim umbra

"It is not fitting to compare, as Calvin does, the Pentateuch with the volumes of Councils and the books of Canon Law; it would be more fitting to compare it with a small Catechism, since a Christian can be saved if he only knows a small Catechism."

-St. Robert Bellarmine
De Romano Pontifice
Book IV, ch. 28.

CHAPTER I

What Christian Doctrine is and what are its Principal Parts.

STUDENT. *So that I may grasp the understanding of Christian doctrine that is necessary for salvation, I especially long for you to tell me: what is Christian doctrine?*

TEACHER. Christian Doctrine is like a short compendium, or a summary of all those things that Christ our Lord taught when He showed us the way of eternal salvation.

S. *What principal parts of this doctrine are most important?*

T. There are four, namely the Apostle's Creed, the Lord's Prayer, the Ten Commandments and the Seven Sacraments.

S. *Why are there only four parts and not a great many more, or fewer?*

T. Because the first three principle parts correspond to the virtues of Faith, Hope and Charity. The Apostle's Creed is necessary for faith itself since it teaches us those things that we ought to believe. The Lord's Prayer is necessary for hope itself, as you see it proposes to us what is to be hoped for. The Ten Commandments teach us those things that are necessary for charity, what we must do to please God. Lastly, the Seven Sacraments are necessary because they are the instruments whereby we might recoup and preserve the virtue which we already said was necessary to salvation.

S. *Would you give a parable through which I may better understand the necessity of these parts?*

T. St. Augustine uses a parable about a house.[2] Just in the way that the placement of a foundation is necessary to the structure of a house, then from there the building of the walls, and next the construction of the roof and different hardware; so also in the structure of salvation it is necessary to lay the foundation of faith, the walls of hope and the roof of charity, and lastly, the hardware which is the holy Sacraments themselves.

---

[2] *Ser. 22 de verb. Domini.*

CHAPTER II
An Explanation of the Sign of the Holy Cross

STUDENT. *Before we begin the first part of this doctrine, I would like you to propose to me what we are obliged to believe, starting with a simple explanation of the accompanying mysteries and also the matters contained in the creed that are more necessary in themselves.*

TEACHER. This is a good question. You ought to know that there are two principal mysteries of our faith contained in that which is called the sign of the Cross. The first mystery is the unity and the Trinity of God, while the second is the Incarnation and Passion of our Savior.

S. *What do you mean by unity and Trinity?*

T. These are sublime matters, and so they must be explained in the progress of this doctrine. But now it will be enough if you would take hold of, and understand these names. Unity of God is merely some matter transcending all created things; He did not have a beginning but always was and always will be; on the other hand, He preserves all other created things as well as rules them; this unity is the highest of

5

all things, the most beautiful, the most noble, and the most powerful, the mistress of all things: it is called God, Who is One, accordingly it could only be one true Godhead, this is, only one nature and essence, infinite power, good wisdom, etc. Just the same, this Godhead is discovered in three persons, namely Father, Son and Holy Spirit, threefold in regard to their persons but in regard to their nature and essence, which is the same, one. I will clarify the matter by an example. If three persons were merely on earth, of which one was Peter, another Paul, and the third, John, and they had one and the same soul and body, they would be said to be three persons because one would be of Peter, the other of Paul, and the third of John; just the same, it would be one man, not three, since neither have three souls nor three bodies, but one body and one soul. Clearly that is impossible among men, since their essence is meager and finite, therefore they cannot be in many persons. The essence of God, however, (since divinity is infinite) the same essence and the same divinity may be discovered in the Father, and in the Son, and in the Holy Spirit. Therefore they are three persons, for one is of the Father, one of the Son and one of the Holy Spirit, still God, although the Godhead has the same essence, the same power, the same wisdom, goodness and so on and so forth.

S. *Now tell me, what is the Incarnation and Passion of Christ our Savior?*

T. This must be known; the second person in the Trinity, whom we name the Son, had a divine nature which He had before the creation of the world, nay more, from all eternity and He took up human flesh and a human soul; that is, He united our whole nature to Himself in the womb of the most chaste Virgin; He who had first been only God, thereafter began to be God and man. After He had lived with men for 33 years, had shown the way of salvation, performed many miracles and finally permitted Himself to be put on the cross and breathed His last to make satisfaction to the Father for the sins of the whole world; just the same he rose on the third day, and after the fortieth day after the Resurrection, He ascended into heaven. We will speak of this more in the explanation of the twelve articles of the Creed. And these things are what the Incarnation and Passion of our Savior mean.

S. *Why is this particular matter a mystery of our faith?*

T. Firstly, because it absolutely encompasses the beginning and the final end of man himself; secondly, because it offers the most unique and efficacious means to know this first beginning and to achieve the final end. Next, through faith and confession of these two mysteries we are set apart from the false sects of the heathen, such as Turks, Jews, and heretics. Next, because without faith and confession of these two mysteries no man can be saved.

S. *In what arrangement are these mysteries understood in the most holy sign of the Cross?*

T. When we make the most holy sign of the cross we say, "*In the name of the Father, and of the Son, and of the Holy Spirit,*" and we sign ourselves in the manner of the cross. We touch our forehead with our right hand while saying "*In the name of the Father,*" next the breast when saying, "*of the Son,*" and lastly, we raise our right hand, moving it from the left shoulder to the right while saying, "*and of the Holy Spirit.*" The phrase "*in the name of,*" signifies the unity of God, for we say, "in the *name,*" not *names;* likewise, it shows the Divine Power that is in the three persons alone. Next, the words, "*of the Father and the Son and the Holy Spirit,*" point out

8

the persons of the Trinity. Moreover, the manner of signing oneself with a cross not only represents the Passion, but consequently also the Incarnation of the Son of God. The progression from the left to the right shoulder (but not from right to left), while using the right hand means we have been transported from transitory to eternal things, and from death to life.

S. *For what reasons would we make the sign of the cross?*

T. First of all, we make it to call to witness that we are Christians, *i.e.* soldiers of Christ our General, and thus it is a specific symbol and becomes like a banner by which the soldiers of Christ are distinguished from the enemies of the Church, such as pagans, Jews, Turks and Heretics. Secondly, we make this sign of the cross to invoke the Divine Assistance in all of our actions. For by this sign we invoke the most Holy Trinity through the merits of the passion of Christ our Savior. For this reason good Christians customarily make this sign when they rise from bed, or leave a house, or sit down for a meal, or leave the table, or when they undertake some business that must be made ready.[3] Lastly, this sign is made so that we will be armed against diabolic temptations. The devil is certainly very scared of this sign, and he flees from it like criminals when they see the torture chamber.[4] Therefore, by the sign of the cross a man is very often freed from many dangers both spiritual and temporal, if he exercises the use of it with true faith and is equipped with confidence in the mercy of God and the merits of our Lord Jesus Christ.

---

[3] Tertullian, *de Corona militis*, cap. 3.
[4] St. Augustine, *lib*. 8: qu. 79; Chrysostom, Homily 53 in Matth.

CHAPTER III
Explanation of the Creed, that is, of the Twelve Articles.

STUDENT. *Now let us come to the first part of Christian Doctrine, for I want to learn more about the Apostles' Creed.*

TEACHER. The Apostle's Creed contains twelve parts, which we call *articles*, and they are twelve for the number of Apostles who composed it.[5] These are:

1. I believe in God the Father Almighty, Creator of Heaven and earth.
2. And in Jesus Christ, His only begotten Son our Lord.
3. Who was conceived of the Holy Spirit, born of the Virgin Mary.
4. Suffered under Pontius Pilate, was crucified, died and was buried.
5. He descended into hell, on the third day He rose from the dead.
6. He ascended into Heaven, and is seated at the right hand of God the Father Almighty.

---

[5] Leo, ep. 17 ad Pulcheriam

7. From thence He will return to judge the living and the dead.
8. I believe in the Holy Spirit,
9. The Holy Catholic Church, the communion of Saints,
10. The remission of sins,
11. The resurrection of the body,
12. And life everlasting. Amen.

EXPLANATION OF THE FIRST ARTICLE

S. *Explain to me the first article in more detail, starting with* "I believe".

T. It is just as much as if one were to say, I believe firmly and without question all the things which are contained in these twelve articles. Therefore, what God Himself taught His Apostles, which the Apostles handed on to the Church, and at length the Church has passed the same thing on to us. Therefore I believe the articles more firmly than what I see with my eye or touch with my hands.

S. *What does it mean when it says* "in God"?

T. It is the same thing as if one were to say that one must firmly believe that there is one God, even if we do not use our bodily eyes. That God is one, for which reason it says "I believe in God," and not "I believe in a god". Nor should one think that God is like some corporeal thing, however big and beautiful you may like, but rather, one should imagine that God is a spiritual thing, which always was and is always going to be; He created all of those things which exist, and in like manner, fills all things, governs all things, and knows and sees all things. Lastly, anything represented either to the eyes, or in your imagination, if you were compelled to speak about it then what is represented to me is not God because He is infinitely better.

S. *Why is God called* "the Father"?

T. Because He really is the Father of His only begotten Son, on which the second article treats; thereupon, because He is the Father of all good men, not by nature but by adoption; next, because He is the Father of all creatures, not by nature or adoption but by creation, just as we will say in the second article.

S. *Why do you say* "Almighty"?

15

T. Because there is only one from the Divine Names proper to God, and although there are many of this kind, such as Eternal, Immense, Infinite, etc., just the same, in this place, He is most suitably called *Almighty*, that way we do not run into difficulty in the creed that He made the heavens and the earth from nothing; in the same way it appears from the following words. Certainly nothing can be difficult to the One who makes whatever He wants, and therefore He is *Almighty*. But if someone would say that God cannot die or sin, so He can't really do everything; then I answer that to die and sin are not in potency, but impotency, and if one were to speak about any aggressive soldier you like, that he can conquer all things nor indeed can be conquered by any one, then one has not really detracted from his strength by saying that he cannot be conquered, because to be conquered is not strength but weakness.

S. *What does the name* "Creator" *mean?*

T. It means God created all things from nothing, and only He can return all things into nothing. Now truly angels and men can make and destroy something, and even demons can: but they cannot do that except with pre-existing material, nor can they reduce something into nothing, but only change one thing into another, just as a stone cutter cannot build a house from nothing, but needs stones, limestone, wood and like things for that work. Moreover, he cannot so destroy what he has built that it is returned to nothing, but returned to stones, dust, wood and like things. On the other hand, God alone is called Creator because He alone does not need to create and build something from pre-existing matter.

S. *Why is it said that He is* "Creator of heaven and earth"? *Didn't God also create the air, water, stones, animals, men, and all other things?*

T. By the phrase "of heaven and earth," all those things must be received which heaven and earth contain. Moreover, even if anyone would say that man consists of body and soul, he certainly means also all the things that are discovered in man; obviously veins, blood, bones, nerves etc. Likewise, all the things which are discovered in the soul; clearly the intellect, will, memory, interior and exterior senses, etc. So by the name of "heaven" the air, birds of the sky, clouds and stars of the heavens are embraced and at length, angels. But by the name of earth all of those things are embraced that deal with the earth, such as the waters of the sea and rivers, which are constituted in the lowest parts of the earth, and above all, animals, grass, stones, metals, and all things embraced by the earth or the lap of the sea. Therefore, God is the Creator of heaven and earth because these are the two principal parts of the world. Indeed the higher one is where the Angels dwell, while the lower is the one in which men live. Now, since these are the principal creatures, whom all the rest serve, just the same both (to the extent that they were created *ex nihilo* and were exalted to such a dignity) are obliged to serve God.

EXPLANATION OF THE SECOND ARTICLE

S. *Tell me now about the second article, namely "And in Jesus Christ, His Son, our Lord."*

T. God Almighty, about Whom the first article treats, has a true and natural Son, Whom we call Jesus Christ. So that you might understand how God begot this Son, take the similitude of a mirror. When someone gazes into a mirror, an image is immediately produced that is so like him that he cannot discover any difference, in as much as it not only reflects his countenance, but even represents individual movements, so that the image moves exactly in the way the man does. Such an image is so like the man without any labor, without time, without instrument yet it is formed suddenly and in a moment in the flash of an eye. Consider in the same arrangement that when God gazes upon the mirror of the Godhead with the eye of the intellect, immediately He forms an image similar to Himself, and because God directs His whole essence and nature to this image (which we cannot do by gazing), therefore this image is the true Son of God, even if our own image which we behold in the mirror is not our son. For that reason you have to gather how the Son of God is God, in the same way as the Father is God and the same God with God, because He is has the same substance with the Father. Next, the Son is not younger than the Father, but was always just as the Father always was. Accordingly, He advanced from the only vision of God, and God always saw and regarded Himself. At length, the Son of God was not begotten in time from the cooperation of a woman, nor from vicious lust, or from other related imperfections, but only by God, only, as was said, from his vision and by the most pure eye of the Divine Intellect.

S. *Why is this Son of God called Jesus Christ?*

19

T. The name of Jesus means Savior, while Christ, because it is the last name, means High Priest and King of Kings, as we touched upon in the explanation of the sign of the Cross, that the Son of God became man to redeem us in His blood and to restore us to eternal salvation. Therefore, after He became man, He took this name of Savior to himself, to show that He came to save man. He was also given the title of High Priest and Supreme King by the Father, all of which this name Christ designates, and by such a name we are called Christians.

S. *Why do we remove our hat or genuflect whenever the name of Jesus is said, but we do not do this after we hear the name "God"?*

T. The reason is because this name is proper to the Son of God, since all the rest are common; likewise, we are taught by this name how God, by becoming a man for our sake, humbled Himself. Furthermore, we genuflect in an Act of Thanksgiving when we hear this name. Not only do we men genuflect, but even the angels of God in heaven, and the demons in hell, on account of this name the former from voluntary love, the latter are compelled by fear. God also willed that all rational creatures should genuflect in the presence of His Son, seeing that He Himself so bent Himself and humbled Himself even to the death of the Cross.

S. *Why is Jesus Christ called Our Lord?*

T. Because He, together with the Father, created us, and therefore He is our Patron and Lord just as the Father. More to the point, He freed us from the power and captivity of the devil by bitter torments and His Passion, which we will speak of in a little while.

EXPLANATION OF THE THIRD ARTICLE

S. *It follows that the third Article must be explained. What does it mean, "Who was conceived by the Holy Spirit and born from the Virgin Mary?"*

T. By this article the extraordinary and admirable manner of the Incarnation of the Son of God is explained. You know all men are born from their father and mother, and the mother does not remain a virgin, and after she conceives she bears a son; but on the other hand, after the Son of God was incarnate, He refused a Father in regard to relation, but only had a unique mother, Mary, who always remained an inviolate Virgin. For the Holy Spirit, Who is the third person in the Godhead, and one and the same God with the Father and the Son, for His infinite Omnipotence, from the purest blood of this Virgin created the body of the most perfect Infant, and in the same moment He created that most noble soul and united it with the body of this Infant; and all these the Son of God took in His Person; to such an extent that Jesus Christ, Who before was only God, at length began to be a man, and in the same way whereby God had a Father without a Mother, so by that manner the man had a Mother without a Father.

S. *I would be happy if I could understand by some example or similitude by what arrangement a Virgin could conceive?*

T. The secret mysteries of God, even if they are not understood, nevertheless must be believed. For there are a great many things God can do which we cannot comprehend by our genius, therefore in the beginning of the Creed it was said that God is Almighty. Moreover, we have a handsome example in the creation of this world. You know the earth does not ordinarily produce on its own, if beforehand it was not plowed and not planted, or soaked with rain or burned by the sun; just the same, in the beginning when it first produced grain, the earth was not plowed, nor planted, nor warmed and thus (in that manner of speaking) it was altogether virgin; and only from the command of Almighty God through the power of the same God, at that very moment, it produced wheat and grain. So the virginal womb of Mary, without any human commerce, solely from the command of God, by the operation of the Holy Spirit, produced that most precious grain, clearly the animated body of the Son of God.

S. *Seeing that Jesus Christ was conceived by the Holy Ghost, I reckon it can be suitably said that the Holy Spirit is His Father in regard to His humanity?*

T. That is not so, since to be some father of something it does not suffice to make something, but to make it from one's own substance. Therefore we say that the stonecutter is not the father of the house that he made, accordingly he constructed it from stone not his own flesh. Well then, the Holy Spirit made the body of the Son of God, but He did so from the flesh of the Virgin, but not from His

23

own proper substance, therefore, the Son of God is not the Son of the Holy Spirit, but is the Son of God the Father in as much as God, because He holds from that Divinity, and is the Son of the Virgin in as much as He is a man, because he received human flesh from her.

S. *Why then is the work of the Incarnation of the Son of God ascribed to the Holy Spirit? Did the Father and the Son also cooperate?*

T. What One Divine Person worked was done at the same time by the other two, because they have the same power and goodness; but just the same the works of power are attributed to the Father, of wisdom to the Son, of Love to the Holy Spirit. But this work was especially proper to love, with which God burns toward the human race. Therefore, it is bestowed upon God the Holy Spirit just as something proper.

S. *Teach me by some example how it comes about that the Three Persons should coincide in the Incarnation but only the Son was incarnate?*

T. If one man wears a vestment and two other men help him to wear it, then all three of them were employed in the work and nevertheless only one wears it. So in the consummation of the Incarnation of the Son of God, three persons were indeed at hand but only the Son of God put on human flesh and became Man.

S. *Why is* "Born of the Virgin Mary" *added in this Article?*

T. Because it hides even this abstruse miracle: accordingly, after nine months the Son of God came out from the womb of the Virgin Mary without pain or detriment to her virginity, while leaving behind no sign of His birth; He did the same thing when, in His Resurrection He left even though the tomb had been closed, and He entered the Upper Room after the doors had just been closed, where His disciples had again gathered and again despaired. For this reason it is said that the Mother of our Lord Jesus Christ remained a Virgin before birth, during birth and after birth.

EXPLANATION OF THE FOURTH ARTICLE

S. *How must we understand those words which follow in the fifth Article:* "He suffered under Pontius Pilate, was crucified, died and was buried"?

T. That article contains the mystery of the Redeemer; this is its summary. After Christ had lived in this world for thirty-three years, and taught us the way of salvation by His most holy life, doctrine and miracles, He was—though innocent—scourged by Pontius Pilate, then fastened to the wood of the Cross on which He died, and he was buried by certain holy men.

S. *Some doubts occur to me in regard to this mystery which I hope you would explain, since I shall know to show myself all the more grateful to God for this benefit the more thoroughly I will understand it. Tell me the reason why, if Christ, is the Son of Almighty God, did His Father not deliver Him from the hands of Pilate, or even, if Christ is the Son of God the Father, why did He not deliver Himself?*

T. Christ could have freed Himself from the hands of Pilate in a thousand ways if He would have liked, nay, the whole world could not cause Him harm unless it were His will. This fact can be clearly gathered from here. He knew long before, and He foretold it to His disciples, that the Jews would seek His death, would seek to mock and scourge Him, and at length would kill Him. Nevertheless, He did not hide Himself from them, but went out all the more to meet His enemies, who, while plotting to seize Him, still did not know Him, so He said "I am," and when they fell at that very moment as though dead,[6] He did not retreat, as He could have, but He waited until they returned to their senses, and rose, and then at length He was as the meekest lamb lead to the slaughter, and no matter how much it pleased them, He permitted it.

S. *Why did Christ, although He was truly innocent, will to be crucified and killed?*

T. Although there are many reasons, the principal one was to make satisfaction to God the Father for our sins. For it is your concern to understand the offence when it is weighed by the dignity of the one offended, while on the other hand satisfaction must be counterbalanced by the dignity of the one making satisfaction, which is clear in this example. If the servant should strike a Prince, it is held as a grievous excess due to the dignity of the Prince; but on the other hand, if the Prince should do that to a servant, it is accounted the least on account of the lowliness of the servant. In like manner, if a servant would take off his hat on

---

[6] John 18:6.

account of a Prince, it is of little weight, but on the other hand, if the Prince would do the same for the sake of the servant, by the force of customary rules, it would be a very great thing. Well now, the first man (as well as all of us with him), offended God, Who is of infinite dignity, and after that offense was committed, He required infinite satisfaction. Since neither a man nor an angel could enter upon such a dignity, at length the Son of God Himself came, Who, as God was of infinite dignity. Since he assumed mortal flesh, He subjected himself in the same flesh by the death of the Cross to the honor of God, and by this arrangement our offense was satisfied by His punishment.

S. *Is there another reason why Christ so willed to exhaust Himself in a bitter death?*

T. To teach us by His example the virtue of patience, humility, obedience and charity, which are the four virtues, attested to by the four points of the Cross. Greater patience cannot be discovered than that which is in one who innocently suffers an ignominious death, nor greater humility than the Lord of all Lords lifted up on the Cross in the middle of thieves; nor was there greater obedience than to prefer death to not fulfilling the command of the

Father to die; at length there was never greater charity than to pay the penalty of death for the salvation of one's enemies. Here, note charity by great deeds rather than words, and it is shown more in His passion than His deeds. For Christ showed us that He most ardently loves us not only in His infinite benefits, but also in His passion and death.

S. *Since Christ is God and Man, as was said before, and as God He was free from all suffering and death, how is it that here we say "He suffered and died"?*

M. Because He is God and man, He can suffer and not suffer, die and not die at the same time. Again, insofar as God is, He can neither suffer nor die, but insofar as He is man, He can suffer and die. For that reason I said that when He was God, he became man to make satisfaction for our sins by the penalty of death in the most holy flesh that He had taken up, which certainly, had He not been made man, He could not have taken up.

S. *Therefore, if Christ makes satisfaction to the Father for the sins of every man, for what reason is it that so many men are damned, and why is it necessary for us to do penance?*

29

T. Christ certainly made abundant satisfaction for the sins of every man, but just the same, it is necessary to apply that satisfaction to Himself for this and for that man in particular. It must be done by faith, by the Sacraments, and good works, especially by repentance, and so a man must persevere in good works and repentance, even if Christ suffered for us and made satisfaction for us. For this reason many are damned, both those who remain enemies of God, or because they refuse to receive the faith, such as Jews, Turks and Heretics; or because they refuse to come to the Sacraments, such as those who refuse to receive Baptism, nay more those who do not go to confession, those that neither contend they do have to wash away their sins by doing penance, nor propose to live according to Divine Precepts.

S. *Still, I would like you to give me an example.*

T. Take this one then. If there was someone who worked very much and by his labor and sufferings, earned a great sum of money that would suffice for him to pay all the debts of the city as well as to put food on every table, but even with this surety, it will not be extended to all unless he would bear witness for them; he certainly (insofar as it were considered for his part), could satisfy for all, nevertheless many of them will remain in debt because of either pride or idleness, or shackled by other evils, or they will seek no testimony or they will refuse to come in sight of the table to receive the money.

EXPLANATION OF THE FIFTH ARTICLE

S. *In the fifth article it is said,* "He descended to hell, on the third day He rose again from the dead," *I desire to know what hell means there?*

T. Hell is the lowest and deepest place in the whole world, that is, the center. Additionally, in many places Scripture opposes Heaven to hell, as if it were the highest place to the lowest place. Moreover, in that abyss of the earth there are four distinct caverns, or four great receptacles. One of the damned, which is the deepest; thus it is fitting that the proud devils, and the men that follow them, are in the lowest and deepest place that can be found. In the second cavern, which is a little higher, are those souls who receive the punishment of purgatory and they are found even now. In the third, which is still higher than the first two, are the souls of children who die without baptism;

these are not tormented by the eternal fire, but only the punishment of loss, *i.e.* they undergo the loss of the beatific vision. In the fourth, which is higher than the other three, there lived the souls of the Patriarchs, Prophets and other Holy Men that had died before the coming of Christ. Even if these souls had no need of purgation, nevertheless, they could not enter into glory until Christ had unsealed the gates of eternal life by His death. This is why, as long as they were compelled to stay in that place, which is called the limbo of the Fathers, or the bosom of Abraham, which they lived insofar as they were away from punishment, they could rest in joyful quiet waiting for the coming of the Lord with great jubilation. And thus in the Gospel,[7] we read the soul of Lazarus the poor man was carried to rest in the bosom of Abraham, where he seemed to the rich man to be in a sumptuous feast; the latter, burning in the eternal flame, lifted his eyes and saw Lazarus was in a far higher place, surrounded by great joy and consolation, perceiving the fruit of his suffering.

S. *So, which of these four places of hell did Christ descend to after his death?*

---

[7] Luke, 16:23-31.

T. There is no doubt that He descended to the limbo of the Fathers, and he rendered them blessed on the spot, and lead them to the Kingdom of Heaven. Likewise, in other places of hell also He offered Himself to be seen, by terrifying the demons by His victorious triumph, dismaying the damned as the Supreme Judge, but the souls of purgatory by consoling as the Advocate and Liberator. For Christ so descended to hell as He entered as King to the prison, that He would visit the miserable and show favor to each one.

S. *When Christ was already dead, and His Body was laid in the tomb, the whole Christ did not descend to hell, but only the soul of Christ; so how can it be said that Christ went down into hell?*

T. Although that He was dead to the point that the soul of Christ was separated from the body, nevertheless the Divine Person could not be separated from either the body or soul of the same Christ. From there, we believe the Divine Person of Christ laid with the body in the tomb and the same descended to hell with the soul.

S. *How can it be verified that Christ rose from the dead on the third day, seeing that in the evening of Friday Christ was buried even to the night*

33

*preceding the Sunday on which He rose; would
they not be two whole days?*

T. We do not say that Christ was raised from
the dead after three days, but on the third day,
which is quite true, since it is reckoned that He
was in the tomb on Friday, so the first day was
not whole; then for the whole day of the
Sabbath, which is reckoned as the second day,
and then, on some part of Sunday, which is
counted third. Because the natural days begin
from the preceding evening, in which they
divide the day from the night.

S. *Why did Christ not rise immediately from the
dead, but wish to wait until the third day?*

T. For the reason that He showed by this that
He was really dead; therefore, He wanted to
tarry in the tomb so long as to be able to
sufficiently prove the truth of this matter. This
also must be considered, that in the same way
that Christ lived for 33 years in this life as a
mortal man, so also He decreed that He must
undergo 33 hours under the dominion of death.
So many hours are counted were we to compose
them from Friday evening, on which He was
buried at the twenty-third hour, and twenty
four hours on the day of the Sabbath, and eight

34

or nine hours on Sunday, because Christ was raised after the middle of the night around dawn.

S. *Why is it said of Christ that He rose again, but about others that died, such as Lazarus, and the widow's son, that they were "roused"?*

T. The reason for this is that Christ, being the Son of God, raised Himself, *i.e.* by the power of His Divinity He so united the soul to the body that He rose and began to live again.[8] But of others that died, since they could not return to life by their own power, it is said that they were raised by another; just as in the last day of judgment all of us will be raised by Christ.

S. *Is there another difference between the Resurrection of Christ and of those who return to life?*

T. The difference is that these other mortals were raised, and therefore they were going to die a second time, while Christ, being immortal, rose again and cannot again be liable to death.

---

[8] Romans 6.

EXPLANATION OF THE SIXTH ARTICLE

S. *Now we progress to the sixth article, which is about the Ascension of Christ. First I would like to know how long Christ remained on earth after the Resurrection and why?*

T. He remained for forty days, as we can gather from the days which fall from the feast of the Resurrection to the Ascension. The reason why He lingered so long is that He wanted to strengthen the mystery of His Resurrection with many different apparitions; because that mystery is more difficult than the rest. He who believes that has no difficulty in believing the other mysteries. Accordingly, it was necessary that He died before He rose, and that He was born before He died. So, whoever assents to the Resurrection of Christ, will have scarcely any difficulty believing in His Death and Birth. For that reason, it was not fitting for Him to dwell with His Glorious Body on earth, but in Heaven, therefore anyone who believes the Resurrection of our Savior will also easily believe in His Ascension.

S. *Why is it attributed to Christ that He ascended to Heaven, but it is said about His Holy Mother that she was assumed, not that she ascended?*

T. The reason for this is very easy to explain; Christ, as God and Man, entered Heaven by His own power, while His Mother, since she was a creature (albeit of the greatest dignity), was not brought back to life and assumed to the Heavenly Kingdom by her own power, but by that of the Holy Spirit.

S. *What do those words mean, "He sits at the right hand of God the Father Almighty"?*

T. Take care not to imagine that the Father sits to the left of the Son, or that the Father is in the middle, and the Son at the right, and the Holy Spirit, being constituted in some corporal species, at the left. Really, as the Father, the Son (in His Divinity) and the Holy Spirit are equal, it cannot be said that one is at the right or left in the common manner of speech. But to sit at the right, in this article, is to live in the same glory and majesty, as well as in equal loftiness,[9] and hence, one who sits on either side does not sit in a higher or lower place than the other. Since

---

[9] Gregory Nazianz., Orat. 38 de Nativ. Dom.; Ambrose, in Epist. 82 ad Eccle. Vercell.

this is so, this manner of speaking is best understood by what is said in the Scripture, "The Lord said to my Lord;"[10] there, the Son sits to the right of the Father, but now, the Father stands to the right of the Son, meaning they are of equal preeminence, as we said before. Moreover, in the same way as Christ ascending to Heaven, before all the choirs and orders of Angels and the body of the souls of the saints that He brought with Him, He occupies that place which is the throne of the glory of the Most High; thus, He neither rises above the Father nor sits below Him, but sits at the side of the Father (so to speak) as one who is equal with Him in glory and possesses majesty.

S. *Seeing that Christ is God and man, I want to know whether He might sit at the right of God the Father insofar as He alone is God, or whether insofar as He is Man?*

T. Christ, insofar as He is God, is equal with His Father, and insofar as He is man, is lesser than the Father. Just the same, because He is God and man, there are not two Christs, nor two Persons, but only one Christ and one Person; for this reason, Christ is said to sit at the right of God the Father as both God and Man, and thus

---

[10] Ps. 109 (110): 2.

the humanity of our Lord, *i.e.* His flesh and soul, sits in the Divine Throne to the right of God the Father, not due to its own dignity, but because it is united to the true Person, the natural Son of God.

S. *I ask you to propose this very thing to me by some comparison.*

T. I give to you one of this sort. When a king clothed in purple sits in his royal throne, and all princes of the realm sit in a lower place than the king, the purple of the king is certainly in a higher place than the princes, because it is in the very royal throne. This comes to be, not because the purple is of equal dignity with the king, but because it is with the king, when he is clothed in it, as though united to him; so also the body and soul of Christ sit over all the Cherubim and Seraphim in the very throne of God, not on account of the dignity of its nature, but on account of the union with Divinity, and not only as the purple robe is joined with the king, but more closely and thickly united, namely through that personal union as we already said.

EXPLANATION OF THE SEVENTH ARTICLE

S. "Thence He shall come to judge the living and the dead." *Please, when is that coming of our Lord going to be?*

T. That coming will be at the end of the world; therefore, I want you to know that this world will end at some point,[11] and it will be completely destroyed by a fire (just as what happened in the flood), which will consume everything that is within it. And there will no longer be day or night, nor marriage nor business, nor any other thing that we see now. So also on the last day of this world (which nobody knows whether it is near or far away) Christ will descend from heaven to start the general judgment. And those words, "Thence He shall come," teach us not to believe one who bandies about that he is Christ, and strives to entice us with such an idea as the Antichrist will do at the end of the world. For the true Christ will not come from the desert, nor from an unknown place, but will come down from the highest heaven with such glory and majesty

---

[11] Matt. 24:2; 2 Peter 3; Mark 13.

that nobody could doubt whether it may or may not be true. It will be just like when the sun rises; it breaks out with such a light that nobody can doubt whether it is the sun or not.

S. *Why do we say, "He will judge the living and the dead;" isn't everyone going to be dead and raised again from the dead?*

T. By "the living and the dead" we can understand firstly, the good, who live spiritually in the grace of God, while on the other hand, the wicked, who are spiritually dead through sin. Moreover, this is also true, that Christ is going to come down from heaven to judge the living and the dead in regard to the body. For on that day there will be many dead and also many living found, who, although they live on that last day, and there will be many youths and boys among them, just the same, they will all die in one instant, and in one moment again rise to pay the debt of nature.[12]

S. *I have often heard that he who is dead in mortal sin shall immediately go to hell, but he who lives in the grace of God, to the purging fire, or to Paradise, so how can they be judged if the sentence has already been imposed?*

---

[12] Augustine, *de Civitate Dei*, lib. 20, c. 20.

T. In the particular death of some man the judgment of the soul takes place as soon as it leaves the body. On the last day of Judgment, the general judgment over all the world will begin. That is indeed for many reasons. Firstly, on account of the honor of God, because many, seeing the happiness of the impious as well as the tribulation of the good, may judge that God does not rightly administer the world. To them it will appear very clearly that God saw and noted all things, and by a just judgment permitted a temporary happiness to the impious so that some of their good works might be repaid for a very brief space of time, but afterwards, He is going to inflict them with eternal punishment on account of their mortal sins. On the other hand, to see just how He supplied the good with temporal punishments, both to castigate them on account of venial sins, and to exercise their patience, since He is going to bestow upon them the infinite treasure of eternal glory on account of their good works. Secondly, on account of the honor of Christ, Who, although He was unjustly condemned in this world and many did not recognize or honor Him, as was just and especially reasonable, so one day is constituted in which the whole world, whether forced, or of its own will, shall acknowledge and honor Him as King and Lord of all. Thirdly, on account of the glory of the saints, who received cruel persecution from the world, all will see that God shall—in the same degree—honor them. Fourthly, to the ignominy and confusion of the proud and the enemies of God. Fifthly, that the body and the soul would receive their judgment—whether of glory or damnation—at the same time.

EXPLANATION OF THE EIGHTH ARTICLE

S. *The eighth article says,* "I believe in the Holy Spirit," *yet what is understood by Holy Spirit"?*

T. The third Person of the Most Holy Trinity is shown here, just as in the first and second article, the first and second Persons are shown respectively. It shows us that the Holy Spirit is neither the Father, nor the Son, but the third Person, proceeding from the Father and Son, and He is true God with the Father and the Son; nay more, He is God Himself, because He is of equal Divinity with the Father and the Son.

S. *Show me some example of this very thing.*

T. Divine matters cannot be shown perfectly by the examples of created, and especially material, things; just the same, let's use a comparison to the sea or a lake. For a sea is produced from a river, as a river breaks out from the font, so that it is pure, and even the same water. So the Eternal Father, like a font, produces the Son like a river, and at length; the Father and the Son, as a font and river, produce the Holy Spirit like some sort of sea; in the same way, the Father and the Son and the Holy Spirit are not three gods but one God.

S. *Why is the third Person of the Most Holy Trinity called the Holy Spirit? Aren't all the angels and the souls of the blessed Spirits also?*

T. He is called God by excellence, since the Holy Spirit, because He is especially Holy, and the Fashioner of every created Spirit and Holiness. Just the same, there are many men who are called fathers and holy either due to their office, or the wholesomeness of their lives, such as good Bishops, priests and religious; likewise, no one is called Holy Father but the Pope, because that agrees with him by an excellence, since he is the head of all, and by his holiness, dignity and office, just as representing the person of Christ, excels all others.

S. *But if the term, Holy Spirit, agrees with God by an excellence, why is He merely attributed as being the third Person? Are not also the Father and the Son holy?*

T. They are all holy, but since the first Person has a name, namely, of Father, and the second, namely, Son, this third common name falls to the third Person, by which He is discerned from the other two. Additionally this should be known; whenever the third Person is called the Holy Spirit, the two terms effect one name, just as one man may be called John Peter, which is one conjunction that designates a name, even if the two names exist in separate forms as John and Peter.

S. *Why is the Holy Spirit always painted as a dove over the image of Christ and His Mother?*

T. By no means must this be considered that the Holy Spirit has a body, or can see with corporeal eyes; rather, He is so painted to explain the effect that He has in all men. Because a dove is simple, pure, zealous and fertile, therefore it is painted above Christ and the Blessed Virgin to help us understand that Christ and the Blessed Virgin were replete with all gifts and graces, and especially with holy

45

simplicity, purity, zeal for souls and spiritual fertility, whereby they acquired numberless sons, namely the faithful and all good Christians.

S. *Why is the Holy Spirit painted in the form of tongues of fire over the Apostles?*

T. Because the Holy Spirit descended on the tenth day after the Lord's Ascension and filled them with all wisdom, love and mercy, and each was bestowed with a tongue for speaking so as to disseminate faith through the whole world by preaching. Therefore, as a sign of these admirable effects, these tongues appeared to them. For the light of fire of this wisdom means that they designate the ardor of charity and to the species of the tongue, eloquence. Therefore, the Church annually celebrates one great feast to celebrate what God showed to the Church, called Pentecost, or of the Holy Spirit.

EXPLANATION OF THE NINTH ARTICLE

S. *Why is the ninth article arranged,* "The Holy Catholic Church, the Communion of Saints,"?

T. This begins the second part of the Apostles Creed. The first part treats on God, while the second treats on the Church as the Spouse of God. Just as we believe in God and His Divinity in three Persons, so also we believe in the Church, the one Church which embraces three particular goods. The first of which pertains to the soul, which is the remission of sins; the second to the body, which is the resurrection of the flesh; the third regards the soul and body together, which is eternal life, as we will see in the following articles.

S. *I ask that you explain this to me word for word, and firstly, what is the Church?*

T. The Church is a certain convocation and gathering of baptized men who profess the same faith and law of Christ under obedience to the Roman Pontiff. It is called a convocation because we are not born Christians (like we are born either as Italians, or Frenchmen, or of some other nation). We are called by God, and entered this congregation by Baptism, which is like a door of the Church. Still, Baptism alone does not suffice for us to be in the Church; rather, it is necessary to believe and profess the holy faith and law of Christ just as the pastors and preachers of the Church propose.

47

Furthermore, this alone does not suffice, but it is also necessary for us to be in obedience to the Roman Pontiff as the Vicar of Christ, which is to hold and recognize him as the Supreme Head in place of Christ.

S. *Seeing that the Church is a congregation of men, why are those buildings in which the Most Holy Sacrifice of the Mass and the other Divine Offices are carried out called "Churches"?*

T. This is because the faithful, who are the true Church, are gathered in those buildings to carry out Christian exercises; for that reason they are also called Churches, especially when they are dedicated and consecrated by divine worship. Moreover, we do not speak in that part of the Apostle's Creed on Churches made from stone and wood, but about the living Church, such as the faithful, the baptized and those constituted from the obedience to the Roman Pontiff, as we already said.

S. *Why is it said "in the Church" and not "in the Churches" when many Churches are found in different parts of the world?*

T. Because there is only one Church, embracing all the faithful throughout the world, not merely constituted of the living, but also of those who have lived since the beginning of the world, even to the end of the end. And therefore, it is not only called one, but also Catholic, because in each region or place or time, it extends itself to any of those you like.

S. *Why is it said there is one Church since it embraces the multitude of men?*

T. It is said to be one because it has one head, namely Christ, and in His place on earth, the Roman Pontiff, and because it is invigorated by one Spirit and one and the same law, to the extent that it is called one kingdom, because it merely has one king and one law, even if in that kingdom there are many provinces and many cities and outlying regions are discovered.

S. *Why is this Church called holy when still there are many wicked men in it?*

T. There are three principal reasons why it is called holy. The first is because of its head which is Christ, for He is most holy, in just the same way a man is said to be beautiful because he has a beautiful face, even if he has deformed fingers or some blemish in either his chest or shoulders. The second is because all the faithful are holy by the faith of their profession, for they have the one faith that is the most true and divine, they have the same use of the most holy Sacraments, and likewise, the same most just law, insofar as it commands nothing but what is good, and forbids evil. The third is that some really are in the fullness of the saints, while on the other hand, Jews, Muslims and Heretics and similar groups are outside the Church and cannot really be holy in any fashion.

S. *What does* "The Communion of Saints" *mean?*

T. Nothing other than to say the Body of the Church is united in some way, so that if it is well with one member, it is well with the rest.[13] Although they may live in the most remote regions and are not known to us, just the same, we communicate with them and rejoice through the Holy Sacrifice of the Mass, the Divine Offices and other sorts of good works. Such a communion is not only on earth, but, though especially beneficial to the living through the Sacrifice of the Mass, prayers and good works are also beneficial to those in purgatory, as are the prayers of those living in heaven and the souls constituted in purgatory for us.

---

[13] Ps. 118; Romans 12.

S. *Yet, if that is so, will it be worthless to pray a particular thing for another, or to offer the Holy Sacrifice of the Mass for this or that person in purgatory since good works are common to all?*

T. It is not so, even if the Sacrifice of the mass, prayers and other good works are common in their own way. Likewise, they are more beneficial to those for whom they are offered in particular and rather more for the former, than those by which they are applied.

S. *What will we say on those who are excommunicated? Are they not rendered partakers of the good works furnished by the faithful?*

T. The excommunicated are so called because they are destitute of the communion of the saints, and are branches cut off from the tree, or are members removed from the body, such as a humor;[14] whether by branches or limbs sprinkled about they lack unity. For that reason, you can gather as many as can be who are made excommunicate, but, if one will not have the Church as a mother, they cannot have God as a Father.[15]

---

[14] St. Jerome, in c. 3 ad Tit.
[15] St. Cyprian, *De Unitate Ecclesiae.*

S. *Therefore, are the excommunicated outside of the Church like the Jews and other unbelievers?*

T. They certainly are, but still with this distinction: the Jews and the Muslims are outside the Church for the reason that they never entered it through Baptism, while heretics, who are baptized, for the reason that they forsook the faith, they are outside the Church because they went out of their own will and became fugitives. Therefore, the Church compels them with different penalties to return to the true faith from which they left, just as a shepherd compels the fugitive sheep that left the sheepfold by the crook of his staff to return to it. Furthermore, because the excommunicated are Baptized and have the faith, therefore they entered the Church and do not leave it, rather, they are cast out of it by force just as a shepherd separates a mangy sheep from the sheepfold, and sends it as prey to wolves. Still the Church does not drive out the excommunicated from its mind so that they might remain outside forever, but so that they might be contrite over their disobedience, and in the same way, being humbled, may seek to return to the Church and again be received into the bosom of their mother and the communion of the saints.

EXPLANATION OF THE TENTH ARTICLE

S. *What is the "Remission of sins," which is numbered as the tenth Article of the Creed?*

T. This is the first of the three principal goods that are discovered in the Church. For that reason, it must be known that all men are born sinners and the enemies of God, and always slip step-by-step into worse evil until their sins are taken away by the grace of God, and they are made anew into the sons and friends of God. But know that grace is not found except in the Church, in which the true Sacraments are found, especially baptism and penance, which liberate and deliver men from all the plagues of their soul, *i.e.* sins, just like a heavenly medicine.[16]

S. *Continue to tell me a little more about how good the remission of sins is.*

T. No greater evil is discovered in the world than sin, not only for the reason that all evils of this life and the punishments of the next are

---

[16] Ephes. 5; Titus 3.

borne from it, but also because it makes man an enemy of God. What can be said to be worse, than for a man to be the enemy of He who can do whatever He may wish and Whom no man can resist? Or who can defend that man whom God is enraged against? On the other hand, however, no greater good can exist in this world than to be in the grace of God. For who can harm someone that is defended by God, seeing that all things are in His power? In the chief point, know that in corporal matters life is especially valued because it is the foundation of all other goods, and therefore death is to be feared, which is diametrically opposed to life. Now truly, because sin is the spiritual death of the soul, the remission of sin is the spiritual life of the same soul; you can easily deduce how great a good it is in the Church since remission of sin is discovered in the Church alone.

EXPLANATION OF THE ELEVENTH ARTICLE

S. *What does the eleventh Article, "The Resurrection of the body," mean?*

T. It means the second principle good which is in the Church, and the Remission of Sins will be conferred upon all those on the last day of Judgment that will live again.

S. *Will not others, who are outside the Church and lack the remission of sins, also live again?*

T. Insofar as it attains to natural life, it is certain that all return to it, whether they be good or evil;[17] just the same, the resurrection of the wicked was instituted so that eternal punishments might be enforced, and they lack every good. For that reason this life of theirs is rather more called eternal death than true life; for even the true Resurrection to eternal life is for naught but the good who departed from human affairs without sin.

S. *I beg you to tell me whether these same bodies which we now have shall rise again or whether there will be other similar ones?*

T. There is no doubt that they will be the same bodies that we have now that will rise; if it were others, there would not be a true Resurrection, if the very thing which fell did not rise, then the very thing could not be restored to life, which is death. For this reason the resurrection of the body will happen so that our body shall be

---

[17] 1 Cor. 15; Ambr. *de Fide Resurrect.*; Job 19.

rendered a partaker of either reward or punishment, to the extent that it came into the side of good works or of sin; therefore it is necessary that it be the same body, because otherwise it would merit neither punishment nor reward.

S. *How is it possible to bring back to life a body burned and whose ashes have either been scattered to the winds or thrown in the river?*

T. St. Augustine answers this question.[18] Besides, in the beginning of the Creed it was said that God is Almighty, because He can do what seems impossible to us. After considering that God made heaven and earth from nothing, you can have little difficulty believing that He can return a body that has been reduced to ash to its former state.

S. *Please continue. Tell me in what age and stature we shall rise again, since some die in childhood, others in youth, and still others in old age?*

T. All will rise in that age and stature which we had or are going to have in our 33rd year of life,

---

[18] *De Citivate Dei,* l. 22. c. 20.

in which our Lord rose from the dead.[19] The reason for this is that boys will reach that greatness which, had they attained it, they would have had in their 33rd year. And old men will rise in the flower of their youth at which, when they were 33 years of age, they enjoyed. And if anyone were blind, or lame, or a dwarf, or deformed in any way in this life, he will rise again healthy, whole and provided with every sort of perfection, because "the works of God are perfect,"[20] therefore, in the Resurrection what is necessary to a man will be proper, and all vices or defects of nature will be amended.

EXPLANATION OF THE TWELFTH ARTICLE

S. *What does the last article indicate,* "And life everlasting"?

T. This indicates the perfect and complete happiness of soul and body, and that supreme good and the last end which, to that extent that we are in the Church, we shall acquire.

---

[19] *De Civitate Dei,* l. 22, c. 15.
[20] Deuteronomy 32.

S. *Tell me in particular what might be the good in eternal life?*

T. I will show you this mystery with a similitude taken from the business of this world. You know that in this life men desire a healthy body; elegant, agile, and robust, and likewise, a soul that is wise, docile and erudite in regard to the intellect and adorned with every virtue in regard to the will; additionally, they also desire exterior goods such as riches, honors, powers, desires, etc. Well then, this body will have in eternal life, in regard to health, immortality and impassibility,[21] *i.e.* there will be nothing that can be harmful to it. In regard to beauty and clarity, *i.e.* it will resemble the splendor of the sun. In regard to agility, it will be bestowed with such speed that in one moment it can move itself from one part of the world to another, from earth even to heaven without any fatigue. In regard to strength, it will have such vigor that, without food or drink or sleep or rest, it can pour itself into all things which will be necessary to it and fear nothing. Moreover, in regard to the soul, the intellect will be full of wisdom, for it will see God, the Cause of all things. The will shall be so full of charity and goodness that it will not be able to commit one

---

[21] 1 Cor. 15.

venial sin. The riches of the blessed will be such that it shall lack no thing, since it will possess every good in God.[22] Honor for it will be that the sons of God will be equal with the Angels. Likewise, they will be kings and spiritual priests in eternity.[23] Power will be that they will preside over the whole world with God and will be co-rulers, as well as be able to do whatever they like, seeing that their wills shall be so united to the Divine that they can resist it in nothing. Next, their joy will be ineffable, because every power, both in body and in soul, will be the greatest, suitably accommodated to their objects, so that from there, perfect delight, unending peace and perpetual joy and happiness shall spring forth.

S. *If these shall be common to all, and all only delighted in the same thing, could one person be happier in paradise than another?*

T. More correctly, one who had greater merit in this life will have a greater reward and will be happier; still, there will not be any envy or displeasure among them because everyone will be filled according to their capacity, and they will obtain greater glory in as much as they

---

[22] Luke 20; Apoc. 5.

[23] Augustine, *de Civitate Dei*, l. 22, last chapter.

acquired greater merit.[24] E.g. If a father might have many sons, one of whom is greater than the other in regard to age, and he would give them clothes woven from gold to fit their stature, there is no doubt that the older ones will have a greater garment and one that is more precious, but just the same, all will be content, nor will the younger seek the clothes of the older ones because it will not be well suited to them.

S. *Why is this heavenly glory of paradise called eternal life when even the damned in hell will live eternally?*

T. Life is properly in those things that move themselves, so by that reckoning, waters jumping forth from their fonts are called "living" because they move, while those swampy waters which are stagnant are called dead. So also it is said of the Blessed in heaven, that they have eternal life because they can do every thing, which they will with both their inward and outward powers without any impediment, and at any moment working at their own pleasure. Moreover, the damned in hell, although they live, will never cease to consume themselves; just the same, they are

---

[24] Augustine, *Ibid.*

said to absorb perpetual death, because they are bound by fire and will suffer from torments and act against their will to such an extent that they cannot fail to do what they refuse nor do what they will. But the Blessed in Heaven rejoice in every good work without any admixture of evil, and the damned in hell suffer every evil because they cannot do as they will.

S. *What does the last word,* Amen, *mean in the Creed?*

T. In other words, it is to say "this is the truth," *i.e.* "everything that has been said is true and certain."

CHAPTER IV
An Explanation of the OUR FATHER

STUDENT. *Now that I know what must be believed, I would like to know what I must hope for and seek, and by what means it can be obtained?*

TEACHER. Everything that you ask me is contained in the Lord's Prayer, which we call the *Our Father*, because it shows us those things to ask for and how we ought to ask for them, and that prayer which is the very means whereby we should ask for them.

S. *What indeed is the Lord's Prayer?*

T. It is this: Our Father, Who art in heaven, hallowed be Thy name, Thy kingdom come, Thy will be done, on earth as it is in heaven. Give us this day our daily bread, and forgive us our trespasses, as we forgive those who trespass against us. And lead us not into temptation, but deliver us from evil.

S. *Why is this prayer placed before all other prayers?*

T. Firstly, because it is more excellent than all other prayers, in as much as it was composed by Christ Himself, Who is supreme Wisdom. Secondly, because it is very short and very easy to learn, as well as memorize, and because it embraces all the things which one could ask from God. Thirdly, [25] because it is a very useful and efficacious prayer, in as much as He Who shall take the part of our Judge and Advocate, and therefore knows each thing better; by that understanding, if we wish to ask for something, that is what we must ask for. Fourthly, because it is more necessary than everything else that Christians are obliged to memorize and recite daily. For that reason this is called the daily Prayer, which is recited each day. [26]

S. *Therefore, whenever you are ready, begin to explain the first words, "Our Father who art in Heaven."*

T. These few words are like a brief preface and resemble a preparation to the prayer itself. When we say that God is our Father, we take up a certain boldness and trust to pray. Likewise, by saying "Who art in Heaven," we ourselves

---

[25] Augustine, Ep. 121, c. 12.

[26] Conc. Tol. 4, can. 9; Con. Rem., can. 2; Cyprian, serm. 9; Augustine, *loc. cit.*, c. 7.

call to mind the fact that we ought to go to Him with great reverence and humility, clearly since He is not earthly, but the heavenly Father. Then, by calling Him Father, we hope that in all things that we are going to ask He will oblige us. But by saying that He is in Heaven as the Lord and Protector of the world, we understand that He can do whatever He wills. Lastly, by saying "Father," we agree that we are the sons of God and heirs of Paradise; but in that part, "Who art in Heaven," we show that we are on earth and still have not obtained our inheritance, rather, we live like pilgrims and victors in an enemy land and are especially in need of His help.

S. *Could you explain each word a little bit better for me?*

T. The word, "Father," though it duly suits God as the Creator of all things, just the same in this prayer is attributed to God as the Father of all good Christians by adoption.[27] It is true that even those being converted that are zealous and desire to be sons of God, can say to God, "Our Father;" for they cannot say in truth, "Our

---

[27] Cyprian, Serm. 6; Augustine, lib. 2, serm. in monte, c. 8; Gregory Nyss., Or. 2, de Or. Dom.; Jerome, Epist. ad Damasum, de filio prodigo.

Father," who are not sons of God, nor want to be, nor hold any hope of conversion.

S. *Why does it say* "Our Father" *and not my Father?*

T. We say "Our Father," to show that we are all brothers, and as brothers, we ought to love one another just as we are sons of the one Father. "Our Father" is also said to show that common prayer is better than private prayer, and more fruitful than one man praying. For when all unanimously shall say, "Our Father," individuals pray for all and all for individuals.

S. *Why do we say,* "Who art in Heaven"*? Isn't God everywhere?*

T. We say God abides in Heaven, not as if He were not in every place, but because Heaven is the nobler part of the world in which the Divine Majesty, Power and Wisdom is more resplendent; at length it is there that He permits Himself to be seen by the angels and the Blessed face to face.[28] Besides, it can be said that God is in Heaven because He dwells there with the

---

[28] Augustine, lib. 2, de serm. in monte; Cyril of Jerusalem, *Catech.* 5, Myst.

Angels and holy men who are the spirituals of heaven.

S. *Let us come now to the first petition. What is contained in the words, "Hallowed be They name"?*

T. In this place, "name" means a famous reputation, just as when we say *he has a great name*, because it is known to many; or certainly someone has a good or bad name because they are of good or bad repute; or it is known to many, because either a good man is praised or a wicked one is everywhere castigated.[29] Therefore, to "hallow" (sanctify) the name of God is nothing other than to spread the knowledge and recognition of God through the whole world, and to preserve it holy and inviolate in the mouth and heart of man, as it is in itself. Yet, since there are many unbelievers in the world that do not know God, and many wicked Christians that are found to blaspheme and curse against God, therefore, those who are sons of God are touched with zeal for the paternal honor, and they pray with a boundless desire that His name will be made holy through the whole world, *i.e.* that it shall be

---

[29] Augustine, lib. 2 de serm. in monte; Cassian, Coll. 5; Bernard, Serm. 6 de Quadr.

acknowledged by all and worshiped, praised and blessed as is just.

S. *Why do we ask from God that He be known and praised by men? Wouldn't He be more satisfied were He to ask this from men instead of men from God?*

T. A man cannot know God by himself, nor praise Him. For that reason, it is worked in us, that is, by His holy grace, that we ask that unbelievers and other sinners be converted, and being converted shall begin to know and praise His Holy Name.

S. *Why do we begin this prayer with the petition, "Hallowed be Thy name"?*

T. Seeing that we are bound to love God above all things, and certainly more than ourselves, therefore it ought to be our first and most frequent desire in regard to the glory of God, because we were created and provided with reason for this purpose; that we would know and praise God in Whom our supreme good has been placed, as we will speak about later.

S. *Show me now the second petition, "May Thy kingdom come."*

T. In this petition we ask for our own salvation, therefore, it is in right order when we ask the glory of God right away.

S. *What ought we to understand by the* "Kingdom of God"?

T. The Kingdom of God can be received in a three-fold sense: For God has a three-fold Kingdom, of nature, grace and glory. The Kingdom of nature is that which rules and governs all creatures, so that the Lord will be free of all things. Even if the wicked would continue to sin and not observe the law of God, just the same, God also rules them for when these are seen, He impedes their attempts, and if they wish to sin repeatedly He permits it; still later He will severely punish them, nor is there anyone that can resist His will or do other than what He Himself ordains and permits.

The Kingdom of grace is that in which God moderates and rules the souls and hearts of good Christians by giving grace and spirit, that these would willingly serve Him, as well as seek His honor above all things.

The Kingdom of glory will be in the next life, after the day of the last judgment, because then

God will reign with all His saints over all created things without any resistance; then all power will be taken away from demons and guilty men, and they will be thrown into the eternal prisons of hell. For then death and all corruption, along with all the temptations of the world, and the flesh in which the servants of God are now assailed, will be exterminated; so much so that the Kingdom is going to be altogether quiet and peaceful, consisting in the secure possession of perfect and eternal happiness.

S. *On which of these three kingdoms does this petition deal with?*

T. It does not deal with the first, because that is not going to come, but has already come. Nor the second, because that was dealt with in the first petition, and a greater part has already come.[30] Therefore it speaks on the third kingdom, which is still going to come, and it is awaited with great desire and longing by all those who know the misery of the present life. Moreover, our supreme good as well as glory is

---

[30] Cyril of Jerusalem, *Catech.* Myst.; Chrysostom, in c. 6 of Matthew.

asked for in this petition, both of body and of perfect soul.[31]

S. *If we ask here, for the Kingdom of God to come soon, it will take its beginning after the very last day of Judgment: therefore, do we also ask that this world should quickly be ended and that the last day of Judgment would come?*

T. That is exactly right. Even if the lovers of this world cannot hear sadder news than if the last day should frequently sound in their ears; just the same, the citizens of heaven that abide on earth like pilgrims and exiles long for nothing more. For that reason, (as St. Augustine teaches)[32], just as before the coming of Christ into this world, all the holy Fathers of the Old Law pressed on in the desire for the first coming of Christ, so now all the Saints of the New Law press on in desire for His second coming, which is going to produce perfect happiness in us.

S. *Let us pass on to the third petition. What do the words "Thy will be done, on earth as it is in Heaven," mean?*

---

[31] Augustine, lib. 3, de serm. in monte.; Jerome, in c. 6 Math.; Cassian, Coll. 6.
[32] Sermon 20, in Psal. 118 (119).

T. In these words we ask for the grace to perfectly obey the Divine Commands. Since in the second petition the blessed life is asked for, which is the purpose of man, now it was fitting that we ask the principle means to obtain that end, which is the observance of the commandments of God; because thus our Savior said, "If you wish to enter eternal life, keep the commandments."[33] And because we are insufficient in ourselves to keep all the commandments as is fitting, therefore we ask from God that His will might be done in us; this is, that he might give us the grace to fulfill His law, *i.e.* of perfectly obeying His most holy commandments.

S. *I should like to know whether besides being obliged to fulfill the will of God, while observing His commandments are we also held to conform our will with the Divine Will while He sends tribulation upon us?*

T. We are obliged not to murmur in the least, nor to complain against Divine Providence. Whatever He either sends against us or permits to happen, He does with a good end in mind; this is either to the matter of a greater merit if we are good, or purgation if we are bad.

---

[33] Matth. 19.

S. *Why are the words* "on earth as it is in Heaven" *added?*

T. It should mean that we ought to be prepared to obey God, and to perfectly observe the precepts imposed upon us, with such alacrity and promptness,[34] as much as the angels in Heaven, who admit not even the slightest defect in observing all the precepts of God.[35] It can also be said here that we ask that sinners (signified by the earth), should be so obedient to God, just as the saints, who are signified by heaven, obey Him. Or certainly that the whole Church, understood by the word "earth", should perfectly obey God, just as Christ obeyed Him, Who is understood by heaven.

S. *Let us come now to the fourth petition. What does it mean when it says:* "Give us this day our daily bread"*?*

T. Here we quite reasonably ask for the bread by which our life is sustained, after we ask for grace, which is life itself. For one who begins to live, before all things desires food by which he might sustain life. But notice that in this

---

[34] Augustine, Serm. 109, de Temp; Cyril, *Catech.*, 5, Myst.

[35] Chrysostom, in 6 Matth.; Cyprian, Serm. 6; Augustine, lib. 2, serm. in monte, c. 11.

petition we primarily ask for spiritual bread, which is the food of the soul, and secondarily, the bread of the body, which is bodily food. By spiritual food we understand the most Holy Sacrament of the Altar, which is the heavenly and divine bread that wonderfully nourishes the soul. Likewise, the Word of God, which is proposed by preachers, or drawn out from reading spiritual books, nourishes the same life of the soul in no small manner. Next, we understand Divine Inspirations, prayer, and all those things which either sustain grace which we say is the life of the soul, or they lead to its increase. By the corporal bread we understand everything that is necessary to maintain the life of the body, which the soul uses as an instrument of good works.

S. *Why is this bread called* "our daily bread"*?*

T. Daily bread is the same as the bread necessary for each day, because we do not ask for what is superfluous or curious, but what suffices for the simple sustenance of either the body or the soul for each day, especially since we know that we are pilgrims and guests in this life.[36]

---

[36] Cyprian, Serm. 6; Chrysostom, in c. 6 Matth.

Explanation of the Our Father

S. *Why do we say* "Give us"?

T. So that we might understand that, although we may labor to obtain either spiritual or corporal bread, nevertheless, all of our labor is in vain unless God shall labor with us through grace. Just the same, we often see as many men labor in planting and harvesting crops in the fields, nevertheless on account of the sins of the world, the year's crop will be very sparse.[37] Moreover we ask that God will give us our bread, *i.e.* that, not only might He assist us in that by administering it, but even when we take it to sanctify and bless it so that it will benefit the advantage of soul and body.

S. *Why is the word* "today" *added?*

T. The word *today* means the temporal time of our life.[38] For this reason we ask from God to nourish us with spiritual and then corporal bread in this whole pilgrimage until we will have obtained our heavenly country, where there will no longer be any need of either Sacraments or Sermons, still less corporeal food. It can also be said that we ask from God that

---

[37] Augustine, serm. 135.

[38] Cyril of Jerusalem, *Catech.*, Myst. 5; Augustine, Ep. 121, c. 11.

today He would give us this bread because we refuse to be anxious about tomorrow, since we do not know whether we will live tomorrow. Moreover, Christ taught us not to be anxious even about the present.[39] For that reason, the bread, which is enough for today, is what we ask today; tomorrow's necessary bread we will ask for tomorrow.

S. *From what has been said, I find there is another doubt. If we ought not be anxious even about the present, then it would appear they do badly who provide for a year's worth of grain, wine and other necessary things.*

T. Our Lord, when He taught us to not be anxious for anything but the present, meant nothing else than that we should be free from superfluous cares, which would impede not only prayer, but also those things necessary to obtain eternal life. For that reason, if that care for the future were not superfluous but necessary, as it is when it threatens the aforesaid provisions, then it is not evil to busy oneself in the procurement of things for the future. Rather, such care is for today not tomorrow, for if we would always wait for

---

[39] Matthew 6.

tomorrow, then nothing would ever come into being for us at its proper time.

S. *Now the fifth petition follows. What does* "And forgive us our trespasses [debts], as we forgive those who trespass against us, [forgive our debtors]" *mean?*[40]

T. In the four preceding petitions we asked every good from God, whether eternal or temporal. But now we ask in the three following petitions that we might be freed from all past, present and future evil. There you will easily discover what I said above to be true, that whatever can be asked for is contained in this prayer. Therefore, in this petition we ask that God would deliver us from past evil, that is, from the sins that we have committed. Our Lord, teaching the Apostles this prayer declared that through trespasses [debts], sins must be understood.

S. *Why are our sins called trespasses [debts]?*

---

[40] *We have added a literal translation of the Lord's Prayer from the Latin in brackets because the explanation is dependent on the Latin meaning rather than the Old English. –Translator's note.*

T. For a three-fold reason. The first is that every man offends God by his sins, and so is His debtor, that he would make satisfaction for the offense that he inflicted. Second, because one who sins violates the law of God, although such a law promises reward to those that observe it and punishment to those who transgress it, hence the debtor is a sinner that must pay the penalty noted. The third, is because each one of us is obliged to cultivate the vineyard of his soul and render the fruits of our good works to God; this is why one who does not persevere in good works and much more, one who commits evils in their place, is the debtor of God Who is the true Lord of these vineyards. Seeing that we have all sinned, both in doing what we ought not to have, and by omitting that which we ought to do, then it is right that we day to day pray to God with great humility so that He would forgive our debts.

S. *Why are the words added,* "Just as we forgive those who trespass against us" [forgive those who are our debtors] ?

T. Here, in like manner, for the word *debts* we understand the offenses and injuries brought from our neighbor; and we ask God to forgive us the offenses committed against Him just as we forgive the offences that we have taken from our neighbor. Seeing that one who forgives his neighbor their offenses is more disposed to receive forgiveness for the offenses that he himself has committed against God;[41] so on the other hand, one that refuses to forgive the offense of his neighbor makes himself unworthy for God to forgive his offense. Next, by saying we forgive even our enemies for their offenses, we show that mercy pleases us and that we regard that gift for generosity and a token of a noble spirit; that whenever we ask mercy from God he will not say "Why do you ask me to be merciful when you are the enemy of mercy?" or, "How can you wish that I would be generous to you who reckoned generosity to be the sign of an abject soul?"

S. *Enlighten me about the sixth petition:* "And lead us not into temptation."

T. In this petition we ask for help against future evils, clearly against temptations,[42] through which we fall into sin. Therefore, you would know that here we especially pray to God lest He would permit us to be conquered by temptation. To be sure, because temptations are

---

[41] Gregory of Nyssa, Or. 5 in Or. Dom.
[42] Cyril, *Catech.* 5, Myst.

very dangerous, and victory over them is uncertain, therefore we ask God lest he would permit us to be tried, especially when He sees the devil will be the victor.[43] For that reason, we gather a characteristic proof that it is beyond doubt the devil not only cannot conquer us, but cannot even tempt us, unless God should permit it.

S. *I do not sufficiently understand this manner of speaking, "And lead us not into temptation." It seems this phrase means that God usually leads us into temptation, and we ask Him lest we would do that.*

T. To lead into temptation, or to send into temptation, or to send one into temptation or to urge one to sin is proper to the devil, but by no means is it proper to God, Who pursues sin with the utmost hatred.[44] Just the same, by speaking according to this phrase of Sacred Scripture, where it is repeatedly attributed to God, *to lead into temptation* is nothing other than for God to permit someone to be tempted, or to be conquered by temptation. This is why the sense of this petition is what we have said,

---

[43] Hilary and Jerome in c. 6, Matth.; Augustine, Ep. 121, c. 11.
[44] Gregory of Nyssa, Or. 5; Cyprian, Serm. 6.

namely, that since we recognize on the one hand the weakness of our nature, and on the other the deceit and power of the devil, we pray to God that He would not simply prevent us from being conquered by temptation, but also from being beaten by temptation when He sees that we are not going to be victorious.

S. *The last petition remains,* "But deliver us from evil." *What evil is the word in this petition referring to?*

T. This last petition partly confirms a higher petition and partly places next to it whatever you like, therefore He says, "deliver us from evil," that is, not only do we ask that He would pardon our old sins and preserve us from future ones, but that He might also free us from all present evils. Notice how aptly and wisely Our Lord teaches us that we should ask for freedom from evil in general, but He does not descend to particulars, *e.g.*, poverty, sickness, persecutions and like things; because we frequently think some matter to be good which God sees ahead of time is bad for us, and on the other hand, we might think something bad which God sees is going to be useful for us. For that reason, we ask according to the Lord's teaching, that He would free us from all of those things which He judges are bad for us, or else that these should be favorable or adverse.

S. *What does* "Amen" *mean?*

T. This is a Hebrew term, and just as we have already said, as often as if someone were to say "let this be done," or "this is so," and likewise, "Amen" at the end of the Apostle's creed is just like "this is so," so in the end of the Lord's Prayer "Amen," means "So let it be done, I desire it so, thus I ask that it be."

CHAPTER V
An Explanation of the HAIL MARY

STUDENT. *Seeing that you have explained the Lord's Prayer, I would like you to next explain to me the Hail Mary.*

TEACHER. Since you asked, I will gladly do it, so that you may turn out to be a most devout client of the most Blessed Virgin. This prayer is made from these words: Hail Mary, full of grace, the Lord is with thee; Blessed art thou amongst women, and blessed is the fruit of thy womb, Jesus. Holy Mary, Mother of God, pray for us sinners, now and at the hour of our death. Amen.

S. *Why is the Hail Mary ordinarily added after the Our Father, even more than any other prayer?*

T. It is this way because we have no more powerful an Advocate and Mediator with Christ than His most holy Mother; this is why, after the prayer that Christ taught us has been offered to Him, we turn to His Holy Mother, so that she might assist us with her intercession to obtain all of those things which we have just asked for in the Lord's Prayer. To the extent that it happens in this world, where, after we offer some pleas to a Prince in writing, we usually commend the success of the business to someone who exerts greater influence upon the Prince.

S. *Who composed the Hail Mary?*

T. God Himself composed it, although not by His own mouth, but through the mouth of the Archangel Gabriel and of St. Elizabeth and He taught it to us by our Holy Mother the Church.[45] For those words, "Hail Mary, full of grace, the Lord is with thee; Blessed art though amongst women," the Archangel Gabriel spoke, but only as an envoy of God, and God Himself inspired these words through the mouth of His envoy. Moreover, those words, "Blessed is the fruit of thy womb," were added by St. Elizabeth when she was full of the Holy Spirit, just as Luke the Evangelist witnesses; wherefore, we say the Holy Spirit spoke through the mouth of Elizabeth. All the remaining words Holy Mother Church added, which is ruled and instructed by the same Holy Spirit. This is why it can duly be said that after the Lord's prayer, which Christ the Lord taught by His own mouth, there is altogether no prayer more beneficial, insofar as

---

[45] Luke 1.

it was composed by God Himself and promulgated to us through the mouths of His servants.

S. *Answer me this. Why do we say* "Hail Mary"*?*

T. This is the formula with which we greet her, just as friends, and we make ourselves known to her, and so we ought to make bold to go to her. We use the words of the Angel because we know how greatly she would rejoice to frequently hear that unique good that was conveyed to her by the Angel when we say these words. Besides, she rejoices because she sees us mindful of the Divine Benefit toward grateful benefactors.

S. *What does* "Full of grace," *mean?*

T. The grace of God causes three chief effects in the soul. The first, is that it would blot out sins that defile the soul just like stains. Second, that it should adorn it with gifts and virtues. The third, that it should supply strength to set it about with meritorious works and graces of God. The Blessed Virgin, Our Lady, was full of grace because, insofar as it attains to the first effect, she was never infested with the stain of any sin, either original, or actual, mortal, or venial. Insofar as the second, she had all virtues and gifts of the Holy Spirit in a most perfect degree. Next, insofar as the third, she so exercised meritorious works by the grace of God that she transcended all the choirs of Angels with her body together with her soul.

S. *It doesn't seem like Our Lady has greater grace than other saints, because, often I have heard it said that St. Stephen and other Saints were full of grace from the Holy Spirit.*

T. Even if other Saints are also said to have been full of grace, just the same, the Blessed Virgin had greater grace than all of them because God gave her a capacity for greater grace than any Saint. I will explain it with an example: There might be many vases, one of which may have a greater capacity than the other; if this one were filled with balm, all will be full, and nevertheless there will be more balm in this one and less in the other. The reason is that God gives to men the capacity for greater or lesser grace, based on the sort of tasks which He has prepared them for. Now, since there is no greater task conferred on a mere creature than to be the Mother of God, she had a greater capacity, and thus was filled with greater grace than any other mere creature.

S. *What does* "The Lord is with thee" *mean?*

T. This is the second singular praise of the Blessed Virgin, which means our Lord was present with her from the beginning of her Conception, and governed her, instructed her and preserved her.[46] For that reason, it happened that she never committed any sin by thought, word or deed. This is why God not only adorned her with all graces but also wished to abide in her just as the guardian of so great a treasure.

S. *What is meant by* "Blessed art thou amongst women"?

T. This is the third praise which is attributed to the Mother of God, and it is shown not only that she was full of the graces suitable for a Virgin, but had in abundance those that adorn a married woman, to the extent that she transcends all women who ever they are now, or whoever they will be. The blessing of a married woman is fertility, which the Blessed Virgin did not lack, because she bore a Son more precious than a hundred thousand sons. It can also be said that she is the Mother of nearly infinite sons because all good Christians are

---

[46] Augustine, *de natura et gratia*, c. 3.

brothers of Christ, and consequently, sons of this Mother, although this is not by generation and nature, in the manner that Christ alone is her Son, but through the love and maternal affection which she bears toward us. For that reason she is very meritoriously said to be blessed among all women, because they either have the honor of virginity without fertility, or the blessing of fertility without virginity; it is only by a peculiar privilege of God that joined the honor of virginity with the supreme happiness of fertility.

S. *What does,* "Blessed is the fruit of thy womb Jesus Christ" *mean?*

T. This is the fourth praise that is attributed to the Blessed Virgin, that she is worthy of every honor not only due to herself, but also on account of the Fruit of her womb. Just as the fruit commends the tree itself, so also the glory of the Son redounds to the mother. And because the Lord Jesus is not only true man and blessed among all men, but also God, blessed above all things (as St. Paul witnesses), therefore even His Mother is not only blessed among all women, but even among all created things, both heavenly and earthly.

Explanation of the Hail Mary

S. *Explain to me the remaining words of this prayer.*

T. In the following words the Church repeats the characteristic praise of our Lady, which is that she is the Mother of God, and this shows that whatever she wills, she can ask from the same God. For this reason we pray that she would intercede for us, seeing that we, in as much as we are sinners, need her intercession; and likewise, so long as we live, and especially at the moment of death when we are in the greatest danger, that she would always help us.

S. *Why are we advised to say the Hail Mary three times a day when the bell rings, in the morning, at noon, and in the evening?*

T. So that we might be instructed to turn often to the help of God and the saints, since we abide in the midst of our enemies both visible and invisible; nor is it enough to return to the weapons of prayer in the beginning of a work, but that it must be done even while we are doing it, and all the way through to the end of it. Moreover, there is another mystery hidden in this three-fold ringing of the bell. Our Mother, the Church, wishes us to continually remember the principal mysteries of our Redeemer, namely the Incarnation, Passion, and Resurrection of Christ. This is why she bids us to greet the Mother of God in the morning, in memory of the Resurrection, at noon in the Passion and in the evening in memory of the Incarnation. For just as we are certain that Christ was fastened to the Cross around noon, and rose in the morning, so we believe He took on His human nature at night.

CHAPTER VI
An Explanation of the Decalogue, or the Ten Commandments of GOD.

STUDENT. *Since now the Apostle's Creed, the Lord's Prayer and the Hail Mary have been understood, I would like for you to explain to me the Decalogue, which you said in the beginning is the third principal part of Christian Doctrine.*

TEACHER. It is very wise to wish to learn and understand the Ten Commandments of the Divine Law, since faith and hope without charity and observance of the Divine Law do not suffice for salvation.

S. *Why is it that, when there are so many Laws and Precepts in the Church and in the world, this law containing the Ten Commandments is placed ahead of all the rest?*

T. Many reasons can be presented to show the excellence of this law. Firstly, because God instituted this law in the beginning and wrote it on the hearts of men, then chiseled it onto two marble tablets. Secondly, because it is the most ancient law of all, as if it were the origin and font of all others. Thirdly, because this law is the most general of all the laws that can be found, and it obliges not only Christians, but even Jews and Gentiles, both men and women, rich and poor, learned and unlearned. Fourthly, because this Law is immutable, nor does it admit a dispensation for any man.[47] Fifthly, because this Law above all is necessary for salvation, just as our Lord often affirms in the Gospel.[48] Sixthly, because it was promulgated with trumpets and the greatest solemnity on Mount Sinai, amidst the shouting of angels, thunder and lightning and the presence of God over the people.[49]

S. *Before we come to the explanation of the Commandments in particular, I long to know the real purpose and order of these Commandments.*

T. The purpose of the Commandments is love of God and love of neighbor,[50] since they all teach that one must not offend God or his neighbor; for this reason, they are divided into two tablets, as we said above, chiseled in marble. The first tablet contains the three Commandments declaring our obligation toward God, while the

---

[47] St. Thomas Aquinas, I IIæ, q. 100, a. 8.
[48] Matthew 19:17.
[49] Exodus 20:18.
[50] 1 Timothy 1:5.

second proposes seven Commandments engendering our obligation toward our neighbor. Still, I would like you to know that even if the first merely contains three, and the other seven, just the same, both are equal and clear in Scripture because the first are described in many words, but the second in fewer words. And so those seven Commandments, although they use short words, are equal with the first three expressed more broadly.

S. *Why are there only three commandments on the first tablet?*

T. Because they teach us that we ought to love God in heart, prayer and work.

S. *Why are there seven on the second tablet?*

T. Because one teaches us to do good to our neighbor, the other six to not do evil to the same, firstly to their person, then to their honor, thirdly to their fortunes, and in this neither in deed, nor in word nor in heart.

S. *Let us then move on to the Commandments themselves. Firstly, teach me those words which God wrote on the tablets.*

T. The words are these: "I am the Lord thy God who led thee out of the land of Egypt, from the house of slavery.[51]

1. Thou shalt not have strange gods before Me.
2. Thou shalt not take the Name of the Lord thy God in vain.
3. Remember that thou keep holy the Sabbath day.
4. Honor thy father and thy mother.
5. Thou shalt not kill.
6. Thou shalt not commit adultery.
7. Thou shalt not steal.
8. Thou shalt not bear false witness against thy neighbor.
9. Thou shalt not covet thy neighbor's wife.
10. Thou shalt not covet thy neighbor's goods.

S. *What do the words mean that preface the Commandments?*

T. In those words, we understand four arguments whereby it is shown that God can give a Law to us, and we are obliged to observe it. The first argument is contained in these words, "I am the Lord." Since God is our principal and supreme Lord Who created us from nothing, He can, without a doubt,

---

[51] Exodus 20:2.

prescribe a law for us, his servants. The second is understood by the word "God", in which He shows that He is not only the Lord, but also the supreme Judge and Ruler, and thus He can fashion Laws and punish transgressors. The third is contained in the word, "*thy*" for although we were obliged to obey God as servants do their Lord, or subjects a judge, still we have an obligation beyond this in the reasoning of a pact which we undertook in Baptism. For therein God adopted us as sons, and we in turn choose Him as a Father; just the same, God chose all the Faithful as a people peculiar to Himself, and the faithful took on God for their God and Lord. The fourth is in these words: "Who led thee from the land of Egypt, from the house of slavery." This is because it constitutes manifold obligations, and also the obligation of gratitude. For God delivered us from the slavery of the devil and sin, which was foreshadowed in the servitude to the Egyptian Pharaoh, from which the Jewish people were freed by God.

EXPLANATION OF THE FIRST COMMANDMENT

S. *Now explain to me the first Commandment.*

T. The first Commandment embraces three things. The first is that we are held to acknowledge God as God. Second, that we are not allowed to hold anything else as God. Thirdly, that we are not allowed to make idols, *i.e.* statues or images to hold them as Gods, or adore them.

S. *Explain the first part.*

T. God wants to be held for that which He is, without a doubt, for the One True God. This happens when a man cultivates within himself the four virtues pertaining to the Divine Majesty, this is faith, hope, charity and religion. For he who believes in God acknowledges God for God, *i.e.* for the Supreme Truth; in this, Heretics commit offense, because they do not believe in Him. One who hopes in God, he—in a similar fashion—acknowledges God as God, insofar as he holds Him as the most faithful, merciful and powerful, and trusts that He can and will help him in all necessities. Those who despair of the mercy of God sin against, as well as those who hope in man more than in God, or certainly, trust in man as though he were God. One who loves God above all things, holds God for God, *i.e.* for the Supreme Good. Those men sin gravely against those who love any creature either before God or equally with God, or on the other hand—and more gravely—those who hate God. Next, one who worships God with supreme reverence (which the virtue of Religion teaches), holds God as God because he acknowledges God as the Beginning and Author of all things. They sin against this who hold those things consecrated to God with little esteem, such as Churches, sacred vessels, the Priesthood and like things, as well as those who honor men either more or equally as they do God.

S. *Explain to me the second part of this Commandment.*

T. In the second part, God forbids us to hold any created thing in place of God, against which the Gentiles formerly offended, since they did not recognize the true God, but instead honored and worshiped various created things, such as the sun, the moon or dead men as true Gods. Warlocks and witches sin in the same manner. Likewise, deceivers, necromancers and diviners do the same when they convey the honor that they ought to give to the one God to the devil. Nay more, a great many of these hold and adore the latter as their God, and by his assistance, divine the future for certain or discover hidden treasures, or hope to obtain forbidden desires. And because the devil is the chief enemy of mankind, therefore he wretchedly deceives all these and drives them all enticed into various sins by an inane hope; and then he destroys their soul and many times even the body.

S. *Explain to me the third part.*

T. In the third part God forbids us not only to hold some created thing as a God (as we already said), but also to make something to hold and worship as God. The Gentiles sinned against this because they were terribly blind, that they made idols to themselves from gold, silver, wood or stone, and persuaded themselves that they were Gods; especially because the infernal spirits everywhere secretly entered and spoke through these, and they seemed to move; therefore, men served them and offered sacrifices to them. Because the holy Martyrs refused to do this, they suffered very great fines and were tortured to death.

S. *Is there anything else remaining in this Commandment?*

T. It is certainly that God threatens transgressors of this Commandment with the greatest punishment, but promises reward to those that observe it. After He gave this commandment He added, "I am a strong God, jealous, visiting the iniquity of the Fathers upon the sons in the third and fourth generation of those who hate Me, and granting mercy upon the thousands who love Me and keep My commandments." There, it must be observed that God says He is a zealous God that can severely punish, because He is God and wills that He is regarded by the greatness of His honor and zeal for His justice; besides, He cannot tolerate impiety and injustice. Still, there are those who continually sin against Him, nevertheless they live securely and happily as if God were to take no measures against them; but now you see these are God's responsibility, which He will show in His time.

S. *How is it understood that God threatens to punish transgressors even to the fourth generation, but rewards those who keep His Commandments to the thousandth?*

T. God punishes even to the fourth generation because, although a man may live for a while, nevertheless, since he usually does not see the grandchildren of his sons or the grandchildren of his grandchildren, God does not mean His vengeance to descend endlessly to that man's posterity, but to that which a sinner can attain in his life. On the other hand, He extends His goodness not only down to the third and fourth generation, but also to the thousandth, so if so many things will be given, He promises it is going to be extended, because our Lord is more prone to reward than punishment, because reward and retribution flow from His goodness, and to such a degree that it pleases Him in these: but punishment arose from our sins, and He drags it out against His will, as if He were compelled to due to our sins.

S. *Why are these threats and promises no more than attached to the first divine commandment?*

T. Because this principal command is the most grave of all, and because what is said on that must also be understood about the rest.

S. *I would like to know whether the honor that we show to saints and their relics and images is opposed to this Divine Commandment, because it* *seems that we worship all these things, seeing that we genuflect before them and pray to them just as in the presence of God?*

T. The Church is the spouse of God and the Holy Spirit her teacher;[52] for that reason there is no danger that she would deceive or would do anything or teach that something must be done that is opposed to the Commandments of God.[53] Moreover, that I might respond to you in this particular matter, we honor and invoke the saints as friends of God who can be an assistance to us by their prayers and merits; still, we do not hold them as Gods, nor do we adore them as Gods. It is also not against this commandment that we genuflect in their presence, because that worship is not proper to God alone, but even to creatures, especially if it is offered to loftier ones, such as to the Supreme Pontiff and to kings. In fact, it is in common use in many places for religious to genuflect in the presence of their superiors; for this reason, it is no wonder if we show such worship to the saints reigning with Christ in Heaven, such as we show to certain men abiding here on earth.

---

[52] Ephesians 5:23.
[53] Augustine, *Contra Faustum*, c. 12.

S. *Therefore, why do we say, in regard to the relics of the saints, that even though they exert no influence, nevertheless we pray and genuflect to them?*

T. By no means do we direct prayers to relics, which we rightly know are without sense; rather, we honor them because they were the instruments of those holy souls by which they sent forth both excellent works of virtues and merits of life, and the living and glorious bodies existed in their own times, but now are a precious pledge of the love which they bear toward us even now.[54] Consequently, we pour forth prayers before the relics of the saints, praying to those very saints so that through those very sweet pledges, which we hold, we might remember to call to our minds as we show that we have called to mind the honor expended to them.

S. *Can the same be shown about images?*

T. It is like this: because we in no way hold the images of our Lord, of the Blessed Virgin and the saints as Gods,[55] for that reason they cannot be called idols like those of the Gentiles, for

---

[54] Ambrose, *de vid. Hieron. cont. Vigil.*
[55] Council of Nicaea, 11.

they are merely images which call to our mind
Christ, the Blessed Virgin, and the saints and to
the extent that they are in place of books for
those who do not read, because from these
many Mysteries of the Catholic Faith are
learned, as well as the life and death of many
saints.[56] Nor do we do them honor because the
images are merely made from paper, or some
metal, or however skillfully they are made,
rather because they represent Christ, the
Blessed Virgin or other saints. And because we
know these images lack all life and sense, since
they were made by human hands, we ask
nothing from them. Still, while praying before
them, we implore the help of those whom they
depict, namely, the help of Christ, the Blessed
Virgin and other Saints.

S. *If relics and images of the saints are utterly
devoid of sense, how come there are so many and
such renowned miracles for the sake of those who
commend themselves to such images?*

T. God causes all miracles but often through the
intercession of the Saints, and especially of His
Most Holy Mother, and it frequently happens to
those who invoke the saints in the presence of
Images or Relics of this sort. Nay more, often

---

[56] St. Gregory I, ep. ad Serenum.

God uses relics and images as instruments for miracles of these sorts in order to show that devotion of the faithful toward the saints, as well as their images and relics, pleases Him.

S. *So when someone says that he commended himself to such and such an Image and obtained the desired favor, it must be understood that he commended himself to the Saint whose relics or image was present, and because God, through the intercession of the saint, conferred that grace through the means of the same relics and image?*

T. That is it, and I am glad that you perceived what was said so well.

S. *Nevertheless I would really like to know why God the Father is depicted in the form of an old man, and the Holy Spirit in the form of a dove, but the Angels in the form of winged young men; since God and the Angels are spirits and have no corporeal figure, how can painters depict them according to the nature of men?*

T. When God the Father is depicted like an old man, the Holy Spirit after a dove and the angels in the form of winged young men, it is not done because they are really like that, since, as you duly noted, spirits are incorporeal; rather, they are so painted because they often appear to men in such a species. Furthermore, God the Father is painted according to the character of an old man because in Daniel 7:9 He appeared as such. The Holy Spirit is shown in the form of a dove because in John 1:32 He was seen to rest upon Christ after He was baptized by St. John the Baptist. Then the angels appeared many times in the form of young men.[57] But even here we must observe that many things are painted in a certain form, but they are not that way, instead it is so we might understand that they have specific properties or usually cause certain effects. Thus Faith is painted in the form of a woman holding a chalice in her hand; Charity in the form of a woman surrounded by a few children, even though this does not deceive you into believing they are really women, but virtues. It can be said in the same way that God the Father is painted in the form of an old man to teach us that He is very ancient, *i.e.* eternal and prior to all created things. Moreover, the Holy Spirit is painted in the form of a dove to indicate the works He usually works in us, namely innocence, purity and holiness. Then angels are painted in the form of young men because they are always beautiful and vigorous, likewise winged because they immediately

---

[57] Genesis 18:2; Tobit 5.

show up wherever God has determined they should go, and likewise they are clothed in white with sacred stoles because they are pure and innocent, and ministers of the Divine Majesty.

EXPLANATION OF THE SECOND COMMANDMENT

S. *Let us proceed now to the Second Commandment. What is meant by "Thou shall not take the name of the Lord thy God in vain"?*

T. This Commandment treats on the honor and dishonoring of God that is done by words. It is commanded to honor Him and forbidden to dishonor Him. For that reason, this Commandment can be divided into four ways that God is honored by words and four that He is dishonored by them. Firstly, God is honored by words when we pronounce His name affected by charity, but He is dishonored when we take it in vain. Secondly, we honor Him by swearing oaths, and dishonor Him by perjury. Thirdly, we honor Him when taking vows and dishonor Him by violating them. Fourthly and lastly, we honor Him with invocation and praise but dishonor Him by blasphemy and cursing.

S. *Explain the first part to me.*

T. One use the name of God, the Blessed Virgin and the Saints by speaking simply and do so well or wickedly. For those who more intensely love God frequently remember God and speak about Him; they do this from great devotion and affection, just as it is done in the Epistles of St. Paul, wherein, as often as the name of Our Lord Jesus Christ is read, we know that St. Paul bore great devotion and affection in heart in which he divulged it in speech.[58] On the other hand, there are others who, from a wicked custom, when they are either angry or joke rashly advance the name of God, or of some saint, and in fact nothing else comes into their mind. These certainly act wickedly because in a certain measure they tread the most Holy Name of God underfoot. As an example, even though I will not declare all things by an example, those who do such things are the same as if someone having an exceedingly precious garment should carelessly use it too much, namely in every time and place.

S. Now explain the object of the second part, which treats on oaths.

---

[58] Theodoret, qu. 41 in Exodus.

T. To swear an oath is nothing other than to invoke God as a witness to the truth; to do this well three things must be present, obviously the truth, but also justice and judgment, in the same way that God Himself taught us through the mouth of Jeremiah.[59] And just as by swearing an oath under due circumstances God is honored, so on the other hand, He is exceedingly dishonored if someone were to swear an oath without truth, justice or judgment. One who does this, signifies that God is either not conscious of his affairs or certainly makes him the patron of a lie or iniquity.

S. *Tell me more in particular, what is it to swear with the truth?*

T. For one to swear with the truth it is necessary that he assert nothing under oath other than what he knows for certain to be true; nor can anyone affirm with an oath something to be true which they know is false or that they certainly do not know is true. They do the same that promise something with an oath but do not think to carry it out.

S. *What does it mean to swear with justice?*

---

[59] Jeremiah 4:2.

T. It is simply to promise under oath to do something which is just and right. And therefore, those who swear themselves to avenge injuries inflicted on themselves or to do something that displeases God gravely sin; nor must it stand [revise] or be thought that by such promises one obliges himself to these things in another manner, since no one is obliged to do evil, since the Divine Laws constrain us to not do nothing against them.

S. *What does it mean to swear with judgment?*

T. It is merely to swear with prudence and maturity by considering whether something is unsuitable to invoke God as a witness, unless it is for necessary affairs of great importance, and to do that with great fear and reverence. For this reason they sin who blurt out oaths in some trivial affair or in comedy and jokes. They also incur perjury who have a bad habit of frequently swearing, because it is one of the greatest sins that one can commit. For this reason, both Christ in the Gospel and St. James absolutely forbid us to swear without necessity.[60] The saints assign this reason, that swearing an oath should be a remedy for the weakness of human trust, in as much as men

---

[60] James 5.

113

may believe each other with great difficulty;[61] for that reason it must be used like a medicine which is usually taken as rarely as possible.

S. *Explain to me the third part of this Commandment, which is on Vows.*

T. A vow is a promise made to God in some good matter and for the sake of the Divine Majesty. Here three things must be considered. The first is that a vow is a promise, for that reason it is not sufficient to ratify a vow for it to only have been proposed, much less desired, but it is necessary that an express promise be made by word or at least in heart.[62] The second is that this vow is made to God, Whom vows most properly consider. Therefore, when a vow is made to the Blessed Virgin or to another saint, it must be understood that the vow was principally made to God, but to the honor of the Blessed Virgin or the saints, in whom God dwells in a peculiar and by far more excellent manner than in the rest of His creatures. This is why when a vow is made to some saint, it is nothing other than a promise made to God in memory of that saint which must be honored by

---

[61] Augustine, *de Serm. Dom. in monte,* c. 30; Chrysostom, hom. 36, 27, 28 ad Pop. Antioch.
[62] St. Thomas, II IIæ qu. 88. a. 1.

some sacrifice honoring God Himself in the saint. The third is that a vow cannot be made about just anything, rather about some good and for the sake of God, such as virginity, voluntary poverty, and things of this sort. For that reason one who vows a sin, or some work that does not pertain to the worship of God, or even something good which might be an impediment to a greater good, insofar as he would not do something for the sake of the Divine Majesty thus dishonors God and offends against this Second Commandment. Just the same one would also gravely infringe upon this commandment if he were to make a vow that he does not fulfill as quickly as possible. Because God commands in Scripture that one who begins a vow should not only fulfill it but also do it without delay.[63]

S. *Explain the last part to me, which treats on the praise of God and also blasphemy.*

T. In this last part of the Commandment, God commands us not to blaspheme His Holy Name, but rather to praise and bless it. And firstly, in as much as it attains to praise there is no difficulty, seeing that it is manifest that every good proceeds from God and all His works are

---

[63] Deuteronomy 23:21; Eccl. 5:3.

full of wisdom, justice and mercy; it is reasonable in the first place that, in all things, He should be praised and blessed.[64] In as much as it considers blasphemy, you should know that it is nothing other than an injury inflicted upon God by words, either directly or against the saints, and there are six kinds of blasphemy. The first is when something is attributed to God that is not suited to Him; for example, that he has horns or similar inept things. Second, when something suited to God is denied to Him, such as power, wisdom, justice or any other of His attributes, so that if someone were to say that God cannot do this or that, or cannot see, or is not just. The third, is when something that is proper to God is attributed to some creature. Some men do this when they say the devil is prescient of future things or performs true miracles. The fourth, is when someone curses God, His Mother, or the other saints. The fifth, is when someone names some limb of Christ or the saints to inflict injury upon them, just as if they were ignominious things to them, even as these acts are to us. The sixth, is when something pertaining to Christ or the saints themselves is mocked; some do this when they swear by the beard of Christ or St. Peter or

---

[64] St. Thomas, II IIæ, qu 13.

something like it, which are all assailed by the hatred of demons and the perversity of men.

S. *I ask you to tell me how grave a sin is blasphemy?*

T. It is so grave that it is nearly the gravest of all. This can be gathered from the punishment constituted for blasphemies. In the Old Testament, God commanded blasphemers to be stoned on the spot by the whole people,[65] and civil laws punish blasphemers with death.[66] St. Gregory relates about a five year-old boy that had learned to blaspheme; he was not corrected by his father and expired in the lap of his father, and his soul was visibly brought down to hell by demons that had appeared. This is not read about any other sin. For that reason we must very assiduously beware lest we so gravely offend the Divine Majesty. It is not difficult to abstain from this sin, since no usefulness or utility is obtained from it, as is the case with certain other sins. Rather, only damnation comes from it. Although one must never sin no matter what advantage or delight one could ultimately obtain from it.

---

[65] Leviticus 24:14.
[66] Justinian, Novell. 77; St. Gregory, *Dialogue*, book 4, c. 18.

EXPLANATION OF THE THIRD COMMANDMENT

S. *Now that I have understood the first two Commandments, explain the third to me.*

T. The Third Commandment, which is on keeping the Sabbath day holy, is somewhat different from the other Commandments. Moreover, the other two preceding ones and the seven that follow are altogether natural. Those do not only oblige Christians, but also Jews and Gentiles. But this third is on one side natural and obliges all, but on the other side is not natural and does not oblige all. For to sanctify feast days, *i.e.*, to hold some day for a saint, and to especially perform good works in Divine worship, is a natural precept, because natural reason prescribes it and so even in all parts of the world some feast day is celebrated. But on the other hand, the determination of such a day, that this one should be chosen rather than another, is not natural. For this reason the principal feast of the Jews was the Sabbath, but now among Christians it is Sunday.

S. *Why did God command the Jews to observe the Sabbath more than any other day?*

T. There are two principal reasons. The first is
that God fulfilled the creation of the whole
world on the Sabbath: therefore, in memory of
such a benefit, namely, the creation of the
world, He wanted that day to be sanctified.
Additionally, He did this to refute the error of
certain philosophers that said the world was
eternal. By celebrating the day of the world's
creation, they manifestly professed that at some
point it had a beginning. The second reason is
because God willed that, after one had driven
their servants, maids and beasts of burden to
labor for six days, and washed them, then on
the seventh day, *i.e.* the Sabbath, they should
give rest to all; thus the masters learned to be
merciful rather than cruel not only towards
their servants, but even to the beasts of burden.

S. *Why do we Christians not worship on the
Sabbath as the Jews, since the reasons for this
observation were so reasonable?*

T. God changed the Sabbath for us to Sunday
for very grave reasons, just as He changed
Circumcision into Baptism, the Paschal Lamb
into the Most Blessed Sacrament, and all the
good ceremonies of the Old Testament into the
better rites of the New Testament. For, if the
Jews worshiped on the Sabbath in memory of

the created world because creation was completed on that day, then we certainly celebrate Sunday in memory of the same creation, but by a better law, begun on Sunday. And if the Jews offered sacrifice to God on the last day of the week, how much better do Christians do in offering on the first? Besides, on the Lord's day we cultivate afresh three principal benefits of our redemption. For Christ was born on Sunday, He rose on Sunday, and He sent the Holy Spirit over the Apostles on Sunday. Next, the Sabbath indicates that rest which the Holy Fathers had in Limbo; but on the other hand, Sunday shows the glory which the souls of the blessed now possess, and later, their bodies will possess in heaven. Therefore, the Jews worshiped on the Sabbath [Saturday] because after death they descended into Limbo as into a place of rest. But Christians worship on Sunday because after death they ascend to the glory of paradise, only of course, if they do good works and live their lives in conformity to the Law given by God.

S. *Isn't it also necessary to observe other feast days besides Sunday?*

T. There are indeed many other days that must be observed, not only of Christ the Lord but even of the Blessed Virgin and the feasts of other saints, which the Holy Church commands us to observe. But we especially require Sunday because that feast day is the most ancient, and is celebrated more often than the others; just the same, even among the Jews there were many feasts, but the most ancient, the best, and what recurred more frequently than the others was the Sabbath. For this reason, even in the Decalogue, express mention is made of the Sabbath alone, which, as we said, Sunday succeeded.

S. *Then what is required for the due observance of a feast day?*

T. There are two: the first, is that we should abstain from all servile works; clearly those which usually workers and servants do, only from the tiring of the body. For, those works in which the intellect principally labors, cannot be called servile, even if the intellect assists, even if the tongue, the hand, or another part of the body work together. The other, is that we be personally present at the most Holy Sacrifice of the Mass. And although the Church does not oblige us to anything else, just the same, it is still agreeable that on the whole day, or at least a part, we should be more inclined to prayer and spiritual reading, in going to Church, hearing sermons, and carrying out similar exercises of piety. For that is the purpose to which feasts were constituted.

S. *If servile work is not permitted on the day of a feast, then is it allowed to ring the bells, prepare tables or cook food since these are all servile works?*

T. The Commandment to not do servile work must be understood by a two-fold condition. The first, is that servile work must not be necessary for the sustenance of human life, for that reason to cook, prepare table and like things, if they could not be done the day before, are permitted. The second is that they must not be necessary to divine worship. Hence, to ring bells or carry out other things like that in Church, which cannot be done on another day, is permitted. Besides, servile works are permitted on feast days when a Prelate permits them to be done for a reasonable cause.

EXPLANATION OF THE FOURTH COMMANDMENT

S. *The Fourth Commandment follows, which is about honoring our parents; I would like you to explain to me why the Commandments of the second tablet begin with the honor for mother and father.*

T. Just as the Commandments of the first tablet consider God, so the Commandments of the second tablet consider one's neighbor. And because among our neighbors there is no one closer to us, or to whom we are more obliged, than our father and mother, from whom we have life, because it is the foundation of all temporal goods, therefore it is most just that the Commandments of the second tablet begin with the honor for one's father and mother.

S. *What is understood by the honor due to one's father and mother?*

T. Three things: assistance, obedience and reverence. Firstly we are obliged to furnish assistance to our father and mother in their necessity, because assistance is spoken of with honor in Sacred Scripture.[67] For it is very reasonable that sons should strive to preserve the life of those who gave them life. Next, we are obliged to offer obedience to our father and mother, as St. Paul says, "Sons be obedient to your parents in all things, for this is pleasing to the Lord,"[68] *i.e.* in all things which are in agreement with the Divine Will. For if a father or mother were to command something which is opposed to the Divine Will, then according to the command of Christ,[69] one should hate his father and mother, this means, to not obey them or to listen to them, in the same way as our enemies. Next, we are held to show reverence to our father and mother by preserving a special respect for them both in our exterior acts, and what is comparable in honor. God so commanded in the Old Testament that those who would have cursed their father or mother should be punished with death.[70]

S. *I don't understand why God would have commanded sons in the Decalogue to succor their mother and father, but not in turn for the father*

---

[67] Jeremiah 15.
[68] Colossians 3:20.
[69] Luke 14:26.
[70] Leviticus 20:9.

and mother to succor their sons, especially while they are minors and require assistance.

T. The obligation among parents and sons is reciprocal, just as the latter are obliged to assist, obey and revere their parents, so also the former are obliged not only to provide food and clothing for their sons, but also to inform and drive them on to virtue. But love of parents toward their sons is so innate that it is not necessary for there to be another law to remind them of their obligation; on the other hand we very often see sons who do not repay the love of their parents, and therefore it was necessary that some law be imposed which makes them again mindful of their obligation toward their parents. It was not enough for God to impose the mere precept, rather, He willed to call mortal men to its observance with both promises and threats.

S. *Well then, what were these promises and threats?*

T. God joined these words to the Fourth Commandment: "That you might live long in the land which the Lord your God will give to you." In other words: Those who convey due honor for their father and mother will obtain

125

long life as a reward, while those who do not do so, will be punished—among the other penalties already mentioned—by being deprived of a longer life. Such a punishment is very reasonable, since it would be a wicked thing for someone who dishonors those from whom he received life to live a long time.

S. *Must all this that you have said about a mother and father also be understood about others, who have been constituted in that dignity, namely, in the place of parents?*

T. You have considered it most rightly, for this precept ought to be extended to all superiors, both in Church and in state.

EXPLANATION OF THE FIFTH COMMANDMENT

S. *Now explain to me the Fifth Commandment.*

T. This precept primarily forbids murder, *i.e.* to kill men; to kill other animals is not forbidden by this precept. The reasoning for that is that they were created for man and can be killed when it is useful for men. Yet, man was not created on account of other men, but God, and so one man is not the master of the life of another man; for that reason, it is not permitted to kill another man.

S. *Nevertheless, we see thieves and other criminals killed by Princes and Magistrates who really are men, and they are not thought to do evil but good.*

T. Princes and Magistrates are provided with public authority and so kill evildoers, but not as the masters of their lives, but as ministers of God, as St. Paul witnesses.[71] God willed and commanded for evildoers to be punished, and—if they were to merit the penalty—be killed so that the good could abide securely and peacefully. For that reason God gave Princes and Magistrates a sword in their hand to exercise justice, defend the good but punish the wicked. Thus when a criminal is killed at the command of a public authority of this sort, it is not said to be murder, but an act of justice. Therefore, one ought to avoid understanding the proper authority [of the commonwealth] in the Commandment "thou shalt not kill."

S. *Another question just occurred to me, someone wouldn't be forbidden by this precept from killing himself as he is another, would he?*

---

[71] Romans 13:4.

T. Without a doubt he would be forbidden to kill himself because no man is the master of his own life;[72] man was not created for himself but for God, therefore no man can deprive himself of life on his own authority. Although certain saints, lest they would lose the faith or chastity brought themselves to death, still these were peculiar, and does it not seem that they were moved by a clear instinct from God? On the other hand, we cannot excuse others from this very grave crime. One who kills himself kills a man and consequently murders because this is the sin principally forbidden in the Fifth Commandment.

S. *Why do you say "principally"?*

T. Because it not only forbids murder, but also to wound another, strike another, and to inflict any injury you like on the life or person of your neighbor. Christ our Lord also taught us this, when He explained that this Commandment forbids all anger, hatred, indignation, rancor and kindred evil affections, as well as words which usually pave the way to murder; on the other hand, He meant for us to be meek and peaceful, as well as to foster peace and harmony with all.

---

[72] Augustine, *de Civitate Dei*, lib. 1, c. 17.

EXPLANATION OF THE SIXTH COMMANDMENT

S. *What is contained in the Sixth Commandment?*

T. In this Commandment the prohibition against adultery is primarily placed: this is to sin with the wife of another. And because in this world, nothing is esteemed more beyond life of the body than honor, therefore, after the Commandment on not killing, adultery is fittingly forbidden, in which honor is destroyed.

S. *Why do you say primarily?*

T. Because the Ten Commandments are the laws of justice, therefore, in them those sins are primarily forbidden in which injustice is primarily committed, such as adultery.[73] Just the same, other kinds of carnal sins are forbidden, such as *Sacrilege*, which is when this sin is done with a woman consecrated to God; *Incest*, which is with a close relative, *Dishonor*, which takes place with a virgin; *Fornication*, which although it is depraved, still is committed with someone that is free such as a widow or a harlot. Then there are other kinds of more abominable sins,

---

[73] Augustine, qu. 71 in Exodus.

129

which ought not even be named among Christians.

S. *I believe what you have said to be true; still, I should like to know upon what foundation the claim that fornication is a sin rests, since it does not appear that [God] inflicts penalty or injury on one who commits simple fornication.*

T. The foundation of all this is found in the law of nature, in the written law, and in the law of grace. In the law of nature, Judah the patriarch willed a woman named Tamar to be killed, who was his daughter-in-law, for the reason that she had been discovered pregnant in her widowhood.[74] From there it is gathered that in that time, before the Law of Moses had been given, men gathered by an instinct of nature that fornication was a sin. Next, in the Mosaic law, fornication is forbidden in various places,[75] and we also read it frequently in the letters of St. Paul that fornicators are not going to enter the kingdom of God.[76] Besides, it is false that no man is inflicted with a penalty for fornication, because penalty is inflicted, namely on the

---

[74] Genesis 38:24.
[75] Deuteronomy 23:17.
[76] 1 Corinthinas 6; Galatians 5; Ephesians 5; 1 Thessalonians 4; Hebrews 12.

woman whose reputation is destroyed by it, and likewise gives birth to children that are illegitimate. Likewise, it does injury to Christ, because since all should be members of Christ, one who fornicates makes himself a member of a harlot. Lastly, it makes an injury upon the Holy Spirit, because our bodies are a temple of the Holy Spirit, and for that reason, anyone who contaminates his body with fornication, profanes a temple of the Holy Spirit.

S. *Apart from the sins you have called to mind, is there anything else forbidden by this commandment?*

T. All other shameful works are forbidden by this Commandment, which prepare the way for adultery and fornication, such as wantonness of sight, lustful kisses and like things; thus we read in the Gospel that the Lord taught while He was explaining the 6th commandment: "He who looks at a women to lust after her, has already committed adultery with her in his heart."[77] This is why if anyone wishes to flee these sins in earnest, it is necessary that he painstakingly guard his senses and especially, his eyes, through which death enters the soul as if through a window.

---

[77] Matthew 5:28.

EXPLANATION OF THE SEVENTH COMMANDMENT

S. *What is contained in the Seventh Commandment?*

T. The prohibition of theft is contained, that someone else's goods must not be taken against the will of their owner. Certainly the prohibition of theft fittingly follows the prohibition of murder and adultery, because, among the goods of this world nothing is valued more after life and honor, than goods and fortunes.

S. *How many ways can one sin against this Commandment?*

T. Principally in two ways, whereby all the rest are embraced. Firstly, when someone secretly steals someone else's goods, which is properly called theft. Secondly, when those goods are taken openly, just as assassins or thieves do, and it is called robbery. Moreover, although the Commandment seems to speak only of the first manner when it says, "Thou shalt not steal," just the same, it must be received in the second manner, since that which forbids the lesser evil certainly also forbids a greater one.

S. *Which sins are reduced to theft, and which ones to robbery, and are they forbidden by this Commandment?*

T. Those that follow: firstly, fraud in buying and selling; or carried out in similar contracts; these are also reduced to theft because it makes a fraud, he secretly takes more from his neighbor than what is due to him.[78] Secondly, all usury which is exercised in money, with an agreement that one should receive something more than the capital itself, which is reduced to robbery. For one who charges interest clearly demands more than he gave. Thirdly, all who damage their neighbors' property, even if the one inflicting damage profits nothing from it, such as if someone could burn down the house of another, and it is either recalled to theft or robbery insofar as it is done secretly or out in the open. Fourthly, one who does not restore that which he ought also sins against this Commandment just as much as if he would have stolen something, because he detained someone else's thing against the will of its owner. Fifthly, one sins against this

---

[78] Augustine, *qu.* 71 *in Exodus.*

Commandment and commits theft who, discovering something that a man lost, keeps it for himself. I say that someone lost because it is not a sin to keep something that never belonged to anyone, such as gems like those that are usually found in the shore of the sea. Sixthly, it is reduced to theft and also robbery, if someone entrusted with the care of things that are in common use should claim it for his own, in such a way that his neighbors would be left without the use of such a thing which was also theirs.

S. *I would like to know whether theft is a great sin?*

T. All great sins can be called mortal sins since they deprive man of eternal life. But theft has this property, that it leads the thief into ever greater evils. We see that the betrayer, Judas, reached such a point from his custom of stealing from those things that had been given to the common use of Christ and the Apostles that in the end he sold his Most Holy Master. We also see, day by day, men slaughtered by thieves, even if they never saw them and never took up a hatred or enmity against them, but do it only from the desire of obtaining some scanty thing that they have in their possession. But God does not permit that he, who snatches something away from another, should long enjoy the use of the thing, which is seen in Judas who hung himself and in a great many thieves who at length fall into the hands of justice and the executioner.

EXPLANATION OF THE EIGHTH COMMANDMENT

S. *What is contained in the Eighth Commandment?*

T. After we treated on the injuries inflicted upon one's neighbor *ipso facto,* now those follow which are inflicted upon one's neighbor by words. Therefore, the Eighth Commandment forbids false witness, which is one of the principal injuries which can be inflicted upon one's neighbor.

S. *Please tell me whether it is opposed to this precept if someone might say something false that has no detriment to anyone else?*

T. Something is usually said to be false in three ways. Firstly, when it inflicts damage on one's neighbor, as if someone witnesses before a Judge about something, that he stole something

135

or killed someone, notwithstanding that he knows it is false, and this is called a pernicious lie. Secondly, like someone that gives testimony obliging his neighbor, e.g., that he freed the neighbor from some danger, and this is usually called the dutiful lie. Thirdly, if someone neither harms his neighbor nor obliges him, and this is called an idle lie. The first manner is quite properly forbidden in this Commandment, because that testimony is not only false but even unjust and a very grave sin. The other two manners, although they are not unjust, nor are they such grave sins, nevertheless it is at least a venial sin to tell a lie and it is not even allowed for a matter of the greatest importance.[79]

S. *Does this Commandment contain a prohibition of any other matter than lying?*

T. This Commandment also forbids the three sins that are committed with the tongue, and can be reduced to: false testimony on some manner, namely, contumely, detraction and reviling.

S. *What is contumely?*

---

[79] Augustine, *Contra Mend.*

T. Contumely is an injurious word advanced in contempt of a neighbor, as when a man reproaches someone else because he is unlearned, has a small brain, is vile or of ill repute, etc. That is a grave sin, especially when it is done with the intention of harming one's neighbor, as Christ shows when He said in the Gospel: "If anyone will say to his brother, 'you fool', he shall be liable to punishment in the fires of Gehenna."[80] I said when it is done with the intention of harming your neighbor, so if it were for the sake of a joke, or that your neighbor should be warned or corrected, they become just like what a father usually does with his sons, and a teacher with his students, but not that they should be scorned or marked with an injury. Certainly this will not be called contumely, nor will it be a sin, unless possibly it were venial.

S. *What is detraction?*

T. Detraction is the denigration of your neighbor's good name by speaking evil about him. This happens either by speaking evils about your neighbor that are false, or even if they are true but secret and unknown; thus one suffers the loss of his reputation which he

---

[80] Matthew 5:20.

obtained unaware of his fault. Such detraction, as much as it is evil, is still frequent among men, so also it is dangerous and grave; for a good reputation is of greater value than riches; nay more, it is placed ahead of all other things in this life. For that reason it is a grave evil to denigrate the good reputation of another; besides, some remedy can be easily applied to other evils, but the loss of reputation is very difficult to remedy, and he who takes it from another is obliged to its restitution. Therefore, the best counsel is to always speak well about others when it can be done with the truth, or if not then to be silent.

S. *What is a reviling?*

T. Reviling is when someone curses his neighbor, saying "curse you," or making use of curses in any other manner, *e.g.* by uttering curses so that this or that evil thing would happen to them. And this cursing is a very grave sin when it is done from hatred and with the desire and intention to really ignite evils of this sort for your neighbor. But on the other hand, if were done without hatred and without wicked intentions of this kind, but with only with the levity of a joke or if it sets out from the onset of inconsiderate anger, it is a lesser sin.

Still, it is always bad because the Christian is by adoption a son of God, and there ought be no other words in his mouth than blessings.

EXPLANATION OF THE NINTH COMMANDMENT

S. *What is contained in the Ninth Commandment?*

T. The prohibition of longing for your neighbor's wife. Even if adultery is forbidden by the Sixth Commandment, nevertheless, God wished to especially forbid the desire or longing for adultery, to show that these are two separate sins.

S. *It seems that in this precept the desire for adultery that a wife commits with someone else's husband is not forbidden, but only the desire of adultery that a man commits with someone else's wife, because it literally says, "Thou shalt not covet thy neighbor's wife."*

T. It is not so, for the desire for adultery is forbidden to a woman in the same way that it is to a man. For although it is said, "Thou shalt not covet thy neighbor's wife," still, what is said to the man is also understood to the woman;

because "woman" is embraced under "man" just as under a nobler thing. On this point, everyone knows that, at least where the world is concerned, adultery is more infamous for a woman than for a man, just as also honesty and chastity are more praised in a woman than in a man. Therefore, if it is forbidden for a man to desire someone else's wife, it can hardly be in doubt whether it is forbidden for a woman to desire someone else's husband.

S. *I recall that you said above that, where adultery is forbidden, in the same place other carnal sins were forbidden. I would like to know whether this must be understood about desire?*

T. There is no doubt that where the desire for adultery is forbidden, so also is the desire for fornication and of all kinds of lust, because the reckoning of all these sins is the same.

S. *Please, tell me whether every desire for someone else's wife is a sin, even if the consent of the will is not present.*

T. Pope Gregory taught there are three degrees in an evil desire of this sort: 1) Suggestion; 2) Delight; 3) Consent.[81] Suggestion is when the

---

[81] St. Gregory the Great, Resp. ad qq. August., c. ult.

devil puts a foul thought in the soul, to which he applies himself to the certain beginning of the sudden desire; if one resists this sudden suggestion, so that no delight arises then the man does not sin and instead increases his merit with God. But if he should add carnal delight to the suggestion, but still he would not consent to it with reason or the will, then the man would have committed venial sin. Lastly, if he were to join the consent of reason and the will with thought and delight, to the extent that the man notices what he thinks and desires it, and it adheres in him by voluntary desire of this sort, then he commits a mortal sin. And this is what is particularly forbidden in this Commandment.

EXPLANATION OF THE TENTH COMMANDMENT

S. *What is contained in the Tenth Commandment?*

T. It contains the prohibition of longing for someone else's goods, both immovable ones, such as a house and a field, as well as movable ones, such as money, animals, fruits and like things. And perfect justice is preserved in this manner, when one inflicts no harm upon his neighbor by word, though or desire.

S. *I wonder why, after God forbade murder, adultery and theft, that He did not also forbid the desire for murder, just as he did for adultery and theft?*

T. The reason for that is man especially longs for any type of thing because it comes to him appearing as something that is a benefit to him. Therefore, he desires to commit adultery because it confers delight, and theft because it offers utility; but murder holds no connected good and therefore is not desired for itself, but merely so that it can allow one to arrive at adultery, theft or some similar thing. For this reason, even if the desire to kill someone is a grave sin, still God did not reckon that He needed to forbid it in particular, because when He forbade murder itself, it is sufficient to gather that even the desire to kill someone is forbidden. Next, since God had closed up the entry point for the desire for venereal delights and theft, consequently, He also closed off the desire for murder, insofar as ordinarily it is not desired unless it is to attain some delight or advantage.

S. *I would like to know why desire is not forbidden in human laws in the same way that it is in Divine ones?*

T. The reason is obvious. Because men, even if they are Popes or Emperors, still cannot search hearts, but only consider the exterior aspect; this is why they cannot punish thoughts since they cannot judge inward desires. So it would not be just for them to try and forbid them. But God, who knows the hearts of every man, can indeed punish the same wicked thoughts and desires that He forbids in His holy law.

CHAPTER VII
An Explanation of the Precepts of the Church

STUDENT. *Besides the Decalogue, are there other precepts proposed that we must observe?*

TEACHER. Indeed there are, namely the Precepts of the Holy Church, which are these:

1. To be present at the Holy Sacrifice of the Mass on the feast days that the Church commands.
2. To fast during Lent, Ember days and likewise on the Vigils where it is commanded, as well as to abstain from eating meat on Friday and Saturday.[82]
3. To go to Confession at least once a year.
4. To receive Holy Communion at least once a year, during the Easter season.
5. To tithe to the Church.

---

[82] This was the law in Bellarmine's time. For those using the 1962 Calendar, Ember days as well as fasting on Vigils and every day of Lent are still marked as customary but they are not obliged in law, since all Latin rite Catholics are under the 1983 Code of Canon Law, which commands only fasting on Ash Wednesday and Good Friday. –Translator's note.

6. To not celebrate weddings during forbidden times, namely from the First Sunday of Advent to the Epiphany, and from the first day of Lent even to the end of the Easter Octave, that is Low Sunday.[83]

Moreover, I do not think anything more should be said on these precepts, both because they are easy and because we will take them up again when we discuss the Mass, Confession and Communion, as well as Fasting in the explanation of the Holy Sacraments.

---

[83] This has also been abrogated by the current law, though it remains a salutary custom. –Translator's note.

CHAPTER VIII
An Explanation on Evangelical Counsels

STUDENT. *I would like to know further, whether apart from the 10 Commandments there might be any Evangelical Counsels proposed by the same, to establish a more perfect manner of living?*

TEACHER. There are many holy and useful Counsels given by God, the benefit of which is that those that keep them can more perfectly observe the Commandments. There are three principle ones: 1) voluntary poverty; 2) chastity; 3) obedience.

S. *What does the Counsel of Poverty consist of?*

T. In that someone should have nothing that is his own; already beforehand he distributed all his goods to the poor, or certainly dispensed them in common, which is just as much as to give them to the poor.[84] Christ not only taught this counsel with words, but even by example, and the Apostles imitated Christ, as we see all the first Christians of the primitive Church in

---

[84] Matthew 19.

Jerusalem did in that time.[85] Then, all religious bind themselves with a vow to voluntarily observe the Holy Counsel of poverty.

S. *What does the Counsel of Chastity consist of?*

T. In that someone would wish to be perpetually chaste, not only by abstaining from every kind of carnal sin, but even from Marriage. Our Lord taught this by word and example, which the Blessed Virgin, St. John the Baptist[86] and all the Apostles (after they were called to the Apostolate), were called to and they followed it, just as all Religious and those initiated into Holy Orders, make a particular vow of chastity.

S. *What does the Counsel of Obedience consist of?*

T. In that someone renounces his own judgment and his own will, because he is called to renounce himself in the Holy Gospel, and to be subject to a Superior in all things not opposed to God. Moreover, Christ taught the world this Counsel not only by word but also by example, when He obeyed the eternal Father in all things; likewise, when He was still a boy, He obeyed

---

[85] Acts 4.
[86] Matthew 19.

His Mother,[87] as well as Joseph who was His putative father, because he was spouse of His Mother (while in truth he was not His father, insofar as Christ was born from Mary the ever-Virgin). Moreover, this is the third Counsel to which all Religious bind themselves.

S. *Why are there only three principal counsels and not many more, or fewer?*

T. Because these principal counsels are so preserved that stumbling blocks placed to perfection are removed in charity. Of these there are three, namely, the love of goods which is abolished through poverty, then the love of carnal desires, which is abolished by chastity, then the love of honor and power, which is abolished by obedience. For this reason, were a man to have none but these three kinds of goods, obviously the soul, the body and external goods, thus he hands exterior goods to God through poverty, the body through chastity and the soul through obedience, and he offers all these things to God in the custom of a sacrifice, and thus is disposed to the perfection of charity in a better manner insofar as it is possible in this life.

---

[87] Luke 2.

CHAPTER IX
An Explanation of the Sacraments of the Holy Church

STUDENT. *Since the three principle parts of Christian doctrine have been understood, with the inspiration of Divine Grace, it remains that you explain to me the fourth part, which, if I recall rightly, treats on the seven Sacraments of the Church.*

TEACHER. This fourth part of Christian Doctrine is very profitable, and, therefore, it is necessary to learn it with great zeal. Consequently, it concerns you to know that the great treasury of the Seven Sacraments is found in the Holy Church, through which we attain, preserve, and increase Divine Grace, and if we lose Divine Grace through our own fault, we are restored to life through them.[88] For that reason, I have proposed to declare firstly what a Sacrament is, then how many there are, by whom they were established, their type, and other things. Then I will explain what each Sacrament is in particular.

---

[88] Council of Trent, Preface to the 7th Session.

S. *Then, when you are ready, begin to explain what a Sacrament is, for that is what I especially want to know.*

T. A Sacrament is a sacred sign through which God confers grace and at the same time it represents outwardly an invisible effect that is worked in our soul. Truly, if we were of an incorporeal spirit like the angels, God would confer His grace in a spiritual manner.[89] Now, since we are composed of soul and body, God, accommodating Himself to our nature, confers grace to us through the means of corporal action, which communicates an interior effect of grace by exterior similitudes. This is clear in the example on Baptism, which is one of the Sacraments of the Church, wherein the body is washed with water at the very moment in which the Most Holy Trinity is invoked, and through that ceremony God confers the grace of absolution and puts it into the soul of the baptized. Furthermore, by this act He makes us understand that just as that water washes the body, so also grace washes the soul and purges it from all sin.

S. *If I understood you correctly, then I gather that three conditions are required for something to be*

---

[89] Chrysostom, Hom. 38 in Matth.

a Sacrament: 1) is that some Ceremony or external action must be present; 2) that God communicates His grace through it; 3) that its Ceremony or action should have a resemblance to the effect of grace and outwardly represent what it signifies.

T. You've got it, well done. But now it must be added further, that there are seven Sacraments in all, and they are known by these names: Baptism; Confirmation (or Chrism); Eucharist, Penance, Extreme Unction, Holy Orders and Matrimony. Now, the reason why there are seven is that God customarily proceeds, in the way in which spiritual life is given, in an incorporeal manner. In as much as He considers the corporeal life: 1) it is necessary to be born; 2) to grow; 3) to be nourished; 4) if a man becomes sick he receives medicine; 5) whenever one must fight, he must be armed; 6) it is necessary that there be some head that rules all men after they are born and increased; 7) that there would be some to whom the duty to propagate the human race would fall, otherwise, if others were not born to succeed the dead the human race would forthwith go out of existence. In the same way, God also constituted this arrangement in the spiritual life. 1) It is necessary for us to be born in the grace of God through Baptism; 2) Confirmation makes it so that grace will grow and be fortified; 3) the Most Holy Eucharist is given so that grace might be nourished and sustained; 4) that whenever the medicine of Penance is received, the grace lost to the soul will be recovered; 5) that when a man is at the point of death he arms itself against the infernal enemy who attacks us more at that time than in any other time, which is done with Extreme Unction; 6) that there would be someone in the Church that rules and governs us in the spiritual life, which is done by one in Orders; 7) that there would be some in the Church who look to the spiritual propagation of the human race, whereby the number of faithful could be increased in this way, which duty is carried out in the Sacrament of Matrimony.

S. *Who invented and established these very marvelous things?*

T. These admirable Sacraments were invented by none other than Divine Wisdom, and established by none other than God Who alone can give grace.[90] Therefore, Christ our Lord, Who was both God and man, invented and established them. Besides, these Sacraments are

---

[90] Council of Trent, sess. 7, can. 1.

like certain channels by which we derive the virtue of the Passion of Christ. For that reason it is certain indeed that no man can dispense this treasure of the Passion of Christ otherwise than in that way Christ established it.

S. *I ask you to tell me, were there Sacraments in the time of the Old Law, and were they of the same excellence as ours?*

T. In the Old Testament there were many Sacraments, but they were different from ours in four ways: 1) They were more numerous than ours and therefore the Old Law was more difficult than the New Law; 2) There were difficulties in their observance, unlike ours; 3) they were more obscure and therefore few understood what they meant, on the other hand, ours are so clear that anyone can understand them; 4) they did not confer grace as ours do, but they only prefigured and promised it. This is why our Sacraments are more excellent, because they are fewer, easier, clearer and more efficacious than the Sacraments of the Old Law.

S. *Then enlighten me further as to which of these seven Sacraments is the greatest and surpasses all the rest?*

T. They are all excellent and each has a proper excellence. Moreover, the greatest of all is the Most Holy Sacrament of the Eucharist, because it contains the very author of grace and every good, namely, Christ our Lord. On the other hand, if you would consider it under the aspect of necessity, then Baptism and Penance are more necessary than all. Furthermore, if you were to consider the dignity of those that dispense the Sacraments, then Confirmation and Orders are of a higher dignity, because they can be conferred by none but a Bishop; but if you consider the easiness it will be Extreme Unction, insofar as sins are remitted without the mental exhaustion of Penance. Lastly, if you were focus on signification, then Matrimony is the greatest, because it signifies the union of Christ with the Church.

On Baptism

S. *Then let's proceed to the explanation of the first Sacrament, and tell me first off why it is called "Baptism"?*

T. The name Baptism is Greek, and only means "washing", as it does in Latin. The Church wished to retain this Greek name because washing is a very common word, and it is also used in things that are rather vile. For that reason, that this Sacrament should have its own proper name as well as be more honored, it is called Baptism.

S. *What is necessarily required for Baptism?*

T. It is required to know at least three things. Since, in certain cases (as we will say in the proper place), anyone you like can baptize, consequently, it is necessary for everyone to know how it must be done. Firstly, true and natural water is required, which is poured over the person to be baptized. Secondly, it is required that at the very moment in which the water touches the person, the words are pronounced, "I baptize you in the name of the Father, and of the Son and of the Holy Spirit." Thirdly, that the person baptizing has the true intention to baptize, *i.e.* of giving this Sacrament, just as Christ established it and the Holy Church usually confers when She baptizes. So if someone lacked intention, e.g. he only made a joke of the whole thing, or was merely washing the body, it would be a very grave sin and that miserable person would not really be baptized.

157

S. *What effects does Baptism work?*

T. It has three effects. Firstly, that it renews man perfectly by giving him the grace of God, through which he passes from being a son of the devil to being a son of God and from a sinner to a just man. It not only cleanses the soul from all stain of sin, but also delivers it from the punishments of hell and frees it from the fires of purgatory. If anyone should die immediately after Baptism, he would go to heaven on the spot, no different than if he had not committed a sin. The second, that it leaves behind in the soul a certain spiritual sign, or character, which can never be removed from a man. From this it is always known that he was baptized, although should he be condemned to hell, it will be a sign that he was from the number of Christ's sheep, just as in this life men are recognized by a tattoo or a brand, that they were someone's servants, just in the way of animals. This is the reason that Baptism can only be received once, because that character can be no more be pressed upon the soul, nor the effects destroyed. The third is that through Baptism one enters the Church and rejoices in the participation of the goods of the same, just as a genuine son of the Church and he makes the profession that he wants to be a Christian

158

and to obey all those who govern the Church in place of Christ.

S. *Who properly confers Baptism?*

T. The priest, by his own office, and especially because he is the one laden with the care of souls. But if the priest were not present, then it pertains to the Deacon, and in a case of necessity, when there is great danger that the creature will die without Baptism, the duty falls to whoever is there, priest or laity, regardless of whether the latter is a man or woman; still, order ought to always be preserved lest a woman would baptize if a cleric were present, and among clerics, he who is higher by degree.

S. *I marvel that Baptism is conferred upon newborn infants, insofar as they cannot receive what they do not understand.*

T. The necessity of Baptism is so great that if anyone were to die without reception of Baptism, or at least desire for it, he could by no means enter heaven. Because infants are liable to danger of this sort, and can easily die, but still do not have capacities to desire Baptism, therefore it is necessary to baptize them as soon as possible. And although they do not understand that which they receive, nevertheless, the Church supplies that which it responds and pledges for them by means of the godparents, which suffices. Just as by Adam we have all fallen into sin and disfavor with God when we still did not know it, so also it is enough for God if, through Baptism and the Church, we are freed from sin and received in its grace even if we do not yet notice.

S. *Why do we receive it through a Godfather and Godmother, of whom mention was made? What is their duty?*

T. In dispensing Baptism, following the ancient and praiseworthy custom of the Church, a man always assists and is called a Godfather,[91] *i.e.* another father, as well as a woman who is called the Godmother, that is, another mother, and these two, or only one of them hold the infant that is going to be baptized, and they respond for him while the priest asks from the infant whether he wishes to be baptized, believes the articles of faith, and like things. Besides, where the infant has reached adolescence, a Godfather

---

[91] We have used the customary English terms here, but the text only makes sense in light of the Latin words, *compater* and *conmater*, which mean literally: "with the father" and with the mother". –Translator's note.

160

and Godmother are still required to have care of him and teach him the chief and more principle points of faith, as well as good morals, if the parents of the boy were more remiss with him. Lastly, it also must be observed that in Baptism, a Godmother, just as he who baptizes, contracts a spiritual kinship with the one that has been baptized and the Father and Mother the same.

On Confirmation

S. *We have done enough on Baptism. Why don't you begin now to treat on Confirmation, or Chrism, the Second Sacrament.*

T. The Second Sacrament is called Confirmation, because of its effect to confirm a man in faith, just as we said a little while before. It is also called Chrism, which is a Greek name, and means the anointing whereby the forehead of the one receiving this Sacrament is anointed. For, just as in Baptism, a man who is washed with water to cleanse the soul from the stain of sin is shown to be purged by the grace of God, so also the forehead is anointed with Chrism to signify that Divine Grace also unites the soul, and by virtue of this anointing it strengthens

161

and rouses it to make war on demons and boldly profess the Christian faith beyond any fear of torment or death.

S. *When must this Sacrament be received?*

T. This Sacrament must be received when a man attains the use of reason and begins to profess the faith, and it is necessary that he should be strengthened and made firm in grace.

S. *Is there still another effect worked in the soul apart from this Confirmation?*

T. It leaves behind an immovable impression or character as a sign in the soul, which cannot be rooted out, and therefore this Sacrament can only be received once.

S. *Why is it necessary for it to impress another sign on the soul, doesn't the Character of Baptism suffice?*

T. It is not without reason that a second sign is impressed on the soul, because through the first, a man is only known for a Christian and from the household of Christ, but on the other hand, by this second he is known as a soldier of Christ and therefore the mark of the General is placed

162

on his soul, or rather, like soldiers of this world that carry the banner of the Captain on their garments, or wear the insignia of their sergeants. But those who go to hell after they have received this Sacrament are especially ruined, to the extent that it seemed that they had taken up arms as soldiers of Christ by their own profession and by the Sacrament, but later rebelled hideously as traitors do.

On the Most Holy Eucharist

S. *Now explain to me the third Sacrament, and first tell me what Eucharist means?*

T. The term is purely Greek, and it means a thankful memory, or thanksgiving, because in that mystery a memory is made and an action of thanksgiving extended from the most excellent benefit of the most Holy Passion of our Savior, and at the same time, is the true Body and Blood of the Lord, for which we are obliged to perpetually thank God.

S. *Would you explain to me more fully everything which is contained in this most Holy Sacrament, so that after its excellence has been understood, I can venerate it much better?*

T. The host, which is seen on the altar before the Consecration, is nothing other than a modest particle of bread, in a round shape made from delicate matter, but in the highest degree, when the priest whispers the words of Consecration, for the true Body of Our Lord is then found in the host. And because the Lord's Body is living and united to His Divinity in the person of the Son of God, so at the same time, the blood and soul and Divinity itself are found in the body, and so the whole Christ, God and man, is present in it. In equal measure, before the consecration there is nothing in the chalice but a modest amount of wine mixed with a bit of water; but after the consecration has taken place, the true Blood of Christ is found in the chalice. Now, because the blood is not outside the body, therefore the body and soul are in the chalice at the same time with the body, as well as the very Divinity of Christ, and so the whole Christ, God and man is proven to be in it.

S. *Yet I see the host, after the Consecration, retains the species of bread as before, and that in the* *chalice also the species of wine as before. Is that right?*

T. That's right. For the species remains in the host, such as the color and taste of bread, just as they were before; but by no means is the substance of the bread itself the same as it was before, so while it is under the species of bread, it is not bread rather, the true Body of the Lord. You scarcely doubted when you heard that the wife of Lot was turned into a pillar of salt; well then, whoever saw this statue would have seen the species of the wife of Lot, but it was no longer the wife of Lot, but salt, under the species of a vanished woman. In just the same way that her inward substance was changed in this conversion, yet on the outside, she appeared in the species of a woman, so also it happens in this mystery. The inward substance of bread is changed into the Lord's Body, and on the outside, the same species of bread remains as before. The same thing is received in regard to the chalice, the species, taste, color and smell of wine is perceived, still, it is not the same substance of wine for that reason, but the Lord's blood under the species of wine.

S. *It is a great remarkable thing that something so large as the Lord's Body can come about under so* *small a species, such as that of the Consecrated Host.*

T. I certainly affirm that it is a remarkable thing, moreover, it is the greater power of God which can indeed do more than the capacity of our intellect to understand it. So Christ said in the Gospel, when he declared that God can so make a camel, which is an animal that is bigger than a horse pass through the eye of a needle, and he adds: "With men this is impossible, but with God all things are possible."[92]

S. *I ask you to explain to me with some example how it might be possible for the body of our Lord to be able to be in as many hosts as are found in so many different altars.*

T. It is not necessary that we understand miracles of God, rather, it is abundantly sufficient if we believe those things seeing that we are certain that God cannot deceive us. Just the same I will produce an example for your consolation. There is no doubt that we have only one soul, which is in every part of the body; the whole soul is in the head, in the feet, nay more it is even in the smallest part of the body. So is it any wonder that God can see to it

---

[92] Matthew 19.

that the Body of His Son would exist in many hosts? Seeing that one and the same soul, through His power, whole and indivisible can be in so many different members of the body afar off from one another in distant places. It is also read in the life of St. Anthony of Padua that when he was preaching at a certain time in one of the cities of Italy, he was also present at the same time in Portugal by means of Divine Grace, and carried out another good work in the same place. Consequently, if God can now cause St. Anthony to be in two different and separate places in his own species, why is it not suitable for His power to cause Christ to be in many hosts under the species of the same hosts?

S. *Additionally, tell me whether Christ descends from heaven when He is transubstantiated in the host or whether He remains in heaven?*

T. When our Lord is transubstantiated in the sacred host, He does not descend from heaven, but through His Divine Power remains in heaven at the same time as He is in the host. Take the example in our soul: An infant that is a few days old is very small, as one can see, who, if he were measured, would scarcely be more than 12 inches, but truly gets bigger by growing than he was before, and soon he exceeds 24.

Now I ask whether the soul, which before was only 12 inches, left the prior when it made it to the second degree or not? It is certain that it did not leave, or was separated because it is invisible, therefore by retaining the first 12 inches, it acquired the second. So also our Lord did not leave heaven, to the extent that He is in the host, nor did He leave the host to the extent that he is in heaven, rather he is found in heaven and in all those hosts at the same time.

S. *Now that I sufficiently understand what is found in the most Blessed Sacrament, I desire to know what is required for its worthy reception?*

T. Three things are required: 1) The one receiving Holy Communion should have confessed his sins and labor in the grace of God after he prepares to go to the communion of this Sacrament. This is because, among the other reasons why this Sacrament is conferred under the species of bread, is that we would understand that it is given for nourishment and the increase of Divine Grace to the living, not to the dead. 2) That we would be altogether sober and have abstained from all food and drink—even of a little water—since the middle of the night.[93] 3) That we might understand that which we do and have devotion toward so great a Sacrament. For that reason this Sacrament is not given to children or to the insane because they do not have the use of reason.[94]

S. *How frequently are we obliged to receive this Sacrament?*

T. The Catholic Church obliges us to receive this Most Blessed Sacrament at least once a year during the feast of Easter.[95] Just the same, it would be salutary to frequent the sacrament more often with the advice of a Confessor.

S. *Explain to me the fruit which we receive in this Sacrament, as well as the end for which it was established.*

T. Our Lord Jesus Christ established this Sacrament for three reasons. The first, is that it

---

[93] This also reflects the Canon Law in force at Bellarmine's time. This has been abrogated by the current law to one hour prior to Holy Communion, with allowance for water and medicine. *Cf.* Can. 919, §1 of the 1983 Code.–Translator's note.

[94] Bellarmine wrote this for the instruction of Latin rite Catholics, he does not intend to address the custom of Eastern Churches. –Translator's note.

[95] Cap. *Omnis utriusque de poenitent. et remiss.*

be food for the soul. The second, is as the Sacrifice of the New Law. The third, is that it should be for us a Perpetual Memorial of His Passion and a precious pledge of His love for us.

S. *What is the effect that is worked insofar as it is food for the soul?*

T. It works the effect which corporeal food does in the body; for that reason, it is offered to us under the species of bread. Just as bread preserves the warmth of the body wherein the life of the body is placed, so also this Most Blessed Sacrament, when it is received worthily, preserves and increases charity in which the health and life of the soul remain.

S. *What is the effect that is worked insofar as it is a Sacrifice?*

T. It reconciles the world to God, and obtains many benefits, not only for the living, but also for the dead that abide in the fires of Purgatory.[96] It concerns you to know that in the same ways that in the Old Testament they offered many animal sacrifices to God, so in the New Testament, the Sacrifice of the Mass has

---

[96] Chrysostom, in Psalm 95; Augustine, *Contra Advers. leg. et Prop.*, c. 20.

replaced them, in which the most acceptable Sacrifice of the Body and Blood of His Son is offered to God through the hands of the priests, who were prefigured by all the Sacrifices of the Old Law.

S. *What is the effect that is worked as a Memorial of the Passion and a pledge of the love of our Lord bears toward us?*

T. Certainly that we become mindful of the immense benefits and that we ourselves would be enkindled to love Him in return for so great a work of the Beloved. And therefore, just as in the Old Testament, God willed that the Hebrews would not only eat the manna, which He had given them from heaven, but He also willed that they preserve it in some vessel as an ever-flowing memorial of the great benefits that God bestowed upon His people when He led them out of Egypt. So Christ also willed that we should not only consume this Most Blessed Sacrament, but that we should even preserve it on the altar and carry it before us in processions, that as often as we shall gaze upon this we will be reminded of His infinite love for us. Yet, by speaking in particular the Most Holy Mass is a certain universal compendium of the whole life of our Lord, lest we would ever let that slip from our memory.

S. *Now that we have covered that, I am eager to know how the Mass is a compendium of the whole life of Christ; is it because I am so moved to devotion and attention when it happens that I am present there?*

T. I will say it briefly.[97] The *Introit* of the Mass signifies the desire which the Holy Fathers had for the coming of Christ. The *Kyrie eleison* signifies the words of these Patriarchs and Prophets who sought from God the desired coming of the Messiah at such a time. The *Gloria in excelsis* means the Lord's Birth. The subsequent *Oratio* or *Collect* signifies His presentation and offering in the Temple. The *Epistle*, customarily said at the left side of the altar (right to us) signifies the preaching of St. John the Baptist, inviting men to Christ. The *Gradual*, or response to the Epistle, signifies the life arising from the preaching of St. John. The *Gospel*, customarily read at the right side of the altar (our left), signifies the preaching of Our Lord whereby we move from the left to the right, *i.e.* from temporal things to eternal ones,

---

[97] The Rite of Mass as it was in Bellarmine's time can still be seen in the 1962 Missal. –Translator's note.

and from sin to grace, where the lights are carried and the incense is enkindled and the Holy Gospel illumines the whole world, and it was filled with the sweet odor of Divine glory. The *Creed* signifies the conversion of the Holy Apostles and of the other disciples of Christ. The *Secret*, which immediately follows the Creed, signifies the secret plots of the Jews against Christ. The *Preface*, sung in a high voice, customarily ends with the *Hosanna in excelsis,* and it signifies the solemn entry of Christ into Jerusalem which He made on Palm Sunday. The *Canon* which comes after the Preface, represents the Passion of our Lord. The *Elevation of the host* teaches that Christ was lifted up on the Cross. The *Pater noster,* the prayer of Christ hanging on the cross. The *fraction of the Host* shows the wound that was made upon Him by the lance. The *Angus Dei* signifies the weeping of Mary when Christ was taken down from the cross. The *Communion* of the priest signifies the burial of Christ. The chant which follows with great joy shows the Lord's Resurrection. The *Ite Missa est,* signifies the Ascension. The *Final Blessing* of the priest relates the coming of the Holy Spirit. The *Last Gospel* that is read at the end of Mass, signifies the preaching of the Holy Apostles when, filled with the Holy Spirit, they began to preach the Gospel through the whole world, and began the conversion of the nations.

ON PENANCE

S. *Now the fourth Sacrament follows, which is called Penance. Why is this a Sacrament?*

T. Penance means three things. Firstly, it shows some certain power, through which someone is said to suffer due to his sins. Now, the contrary of this is called the vice of impenitence, since such a person does not wish to suffer due to their sins, but persevere in them. Secondly, we say penance is that punishment and affliction that a man takes upon himself so as to satisfy God for the sins he has admitted to. For example, we say one does great penance if he exercises it with much severe fasting. Thirdly, Penance means a Sacrament established by Christ whereby someone that has lost Divine Grace after Baptism, but still sorry for his sins and desires to return to His grace, has his sins forgiven.

S. *In what does this Sacrament principally consist?*

T. It consists in two things: the confession of sin and the absolution of the priest.[98] Christ constituted priests as judges over sins that have been committed by someone that has received baptism, and willed them to have authority in His place to forgive sins, so that, were the sinner to confess them, then it is fitting for them to lay them aside. Therefore, this Sacrament consists in that in the same way the sinner confesses his sins outwardly, and the priest pronounces absolution outwardly, so also God inwardly absolves that soul from the knot of the sin whereby it was bound by means of those words of the Priest, communicates grace to it, and frees it from being liable to hell to which it had thrown itself headlong.

S. *What, I ask, is necessary for the due reception of this Sacrament?*

T. There are three things necessary: Contrition, Confession, and Satisfaction, which are also the three parts of penitence.

---

[98] John 20.

S. *What is required for true penitence?*

T. The hard heart of the sinner is softened, as though it were broken due to sorrow over the offense committed against God. On the other hand, two things in particular are required for contrition, and you cannot have one without the other. The first is that the sinner should really be sorry for all the sins he has committed after Baptism, and therefore it is necessary to examine well, consider all his actions, and be sorry for those things that were not done according to the rule of Divine Law. The second is that the sinner makes a firm resolution to not sin in the future.

S. *What does the Confession demand?*

T. That the sinner would be content not only by his contrition, but also throw himself at the feet of the priest just as the Magdalene threw herself at the feet of Christ, (Luke 7.) and confess his sins with truth while adding and omitting nothing nor intermixing some lie. Second, he must do this with simplicity and not by excusing himself or rejecting fault in any way, or by adding superfluous words. Thirdly, by saying all things with integrity, namely, by not omitting anything because of shame, and likewise by adding in their number and circumstances insofar as he can remember. Lastly, he must confess with modesty and humility, and not tell his sins as if he were relating some history, but he should review what he has done as abominable things unworthy of a Christian, while asking forgiveness for them.

S. *What is necessary for satisfaction?*

T. It is necessary to make repentance in his mind, and willingly receive the penalty that the confessor will impose, as well as to quickly fulfill it, all the while being mindful that God furnishes the greatest grace to him, namely, that He forgives the eternal penalty of hell. Thus he will be content with temporal punishment, which is much less than his sins merit.

S. *Tell me what fruit that this Sacrament conveys.*

T. We take four very great fruits in this Sacrament. First, that God remits sins committed after Baptism and changes the eternal punishment of hell into temporal punishment to be taken on in this life, or in Purgatory, as we already said. The second, is that this Sacrament restores the good works that we had done while we were in a state of and lost through sin. The third is that we are freed from the bond of Excommunication, if perhaps it was connected to that sin. It is important for you to know that the penalty of Excommunication is the most severe, insofar as it causes us to have lost the prayers of the Church, the use of the Sacraments, the life of the faithful and lastly, burial in consecrated ground. Now we are delivered from so terrible a penalty through the Sacrament of Penance by the strength of that authority which Confessors receive from their Bishop or the Supreme Pontiff; although a Prelate that is so empowered, even if he is not a priest, can also release us from Excommunication outside of the Sacrament. The fourth and last fruit is that we obtain, through this Sacrament, the capacity for the treasury of indulgences which the Supreme Pontiffs frequently dispense.

S. *What is an indulgence?*

T. An indulgence is a certain freedom which God uses for His faithful by means of His Vicar, provided that he forgives temporal punishment to them either in whole or in part, which they are bound to draw from either in this life or in Purgatory.

S. *What is required for someone to be able to gain an indulgence?*

T. That a man be in the grace of God, shall confess if he is aware that he is in sin, and to fulfill all the things which the Supreme Pontiff demands when he promulgates the indulgences.

S. *How often are we obliged to receive the Sacrament of Penance?*

T. Holy Mother Church commands each man to go to confession once a year.[99] Just the same, it is necessary for someone to confess as often as he proposes to receive the Eucharist while he is conscious of mortal sin. Likewise, one should confess when he is at the point of death, or hastens to some deed wherein he undergoes the danger of death. Besides, one must carefully consider that it is good to confess frequently and to especially examine one's conscience often, since it can only benefit those who rarely confess with supreme difficulty.

S. *Still I would like to ask one last thing: it remains to discover among those goods that have been done by the grace of God, in which ones do we satisfy for sin?*

---

[99] Cap. *Omnis utriusque de poen. et remis.*

T. All of them are reduced to three principle ones, namely: Prayer, Fasting and Almsgiving, which the holy Angel Raphael taught Tobit.[100] The reason for this is since a man has a soul, body and exterior goods, he offers the goods of the soul to God in prayer, the goods of the body in fasting and exterior goods in almsgiving. The term prayer embraces things such as to hear Mass, to say the Seven Penitential Psalms, the Office for the dead and similar things. The term fasting, also takes up all corporal severities that one inflicts on himself, such as mortifications like hair-shirts, disciplines, lying on the ground, pilgrimages and like things. By almsgiving we understand the duty of charity that a man shows to his neighbor due to the love of God.

S. *What is required to fast well?*

T. Three things are required. The first, is to take food only once a day; the second is to do this around the middle of the same day (and really the later the better); the third, is to abstain from meat as well as from eggs and all dairy products wherever that custom is maintained.

---

[100] Tobit 12.

S. *Is it better to make satisfaction to God by doing these works on his own behalf, or to make himself a partaker in indulgences?*

T. It is better for a man to make satisfaction for himself because, by an indulgence, he only makes satisfaction to God for the obligation of eternal punishment, but on the other, by these works he makes satisfaction to God as well as merits eternal life. Just the same, it is the best of all that a man should have zealous care for each, that he might partly satisfy for himself, insofar as he can do it, and partly make himself a partaker of indulgences.

On Extreme Unction

S. *What is Extreme Unction?*

T. Extreme Unction is the Sacrament which our Lord established to the use of the sick. It is called "Unction", or Anointing, because it consists in that a sick man would be anointed with holy oil while certain prayers are said over him. This is why it is called "extreme" (last), because of all the customary anointings applied in the Sacraments, this is the final one. For the

181

first of these is in Baptism, the second in Confirmation, the third in Priesthood, and then the last is conferred in sickness. It can also be called last because it is given at the end of life.

S. *What are the effects of this Sacrament?*

T. There are three things, of which the first is to remit sins that still remain after the reception of the other Sacraments, such as those which a man cannot remember, or did not know, and since he doesn't know and remember them, he cannot not be sorry for them or confessed them. The second is to refresh the sick and give them comfort at a time when sickness oppresses them and the demons vex them with temptations. The third is to restore the health of the body if it would be expedient to their eternal salvation. These three effects are implied in the oil used in this Sacrament, because oil comforts, refreshes and heals.

S. *When should this Sacrament be received?*

T. On this point there are many that err gravely because they do not wish to receive this Sacrament until they are in their death throes. Rather, the true time to receive it is when the doctors judge a sickness to be dangerous and the human remedies at hand do not suffice. For this reason, he must have recourse to the heavenly remedies at such a point in time. It rather frequently happens that the benefit of the holy oil heals a sick man. For that reason one ought not seek this Sacrament if the danger of death does not appear and much less should one wait so long that all hope of improvement evaporates. This is also the reason why someone given the death sentence by a court is not given the holy oil, since he is neither sick nor has the hope of a longer life.

ON THE SACRAMENT OF ORDER

S. *What is the Sacrament of Order?*

T. It is the Sacrament in which the power to consecrate the Most Holy Eucharist is conferred, as well as to dispense the other sacraments to the people; it is also conferred upon those who receive power of this sort to minister to the faithful in the Divine Office. Moreover, it is called "Order" because in this Sacrament there are many degrees and one is subordinated to the other, such as Priests, Deacons, Subdeacons and other lower orders.

Yet it is not necessary to have a fuller explanation because this Sacrament is not for all, but only for those who are of mature age and such erudition that they need no further instruction in Christian Doctrine, but rather should instruct others.

ON THE SACRAMENT OF MARRIAGE

S. *What is the Sacrament of Marriage?*

T. The Sacrament of Marriage is the union of a man and a woman, representing and signifying the union of Christ with the Church through the incarnation, as well as of God with the soul through grace.

S. *What are the effects of this Sacrament?*

T. Firstly it confers grace so that a man and woman would live well with each other, loving one another spiritually as Christ loves the Church,[101] and God embraces the faithful and just soul.[102] Secondly, it confers grace to instruct

---

[101] Ephes. 5.
[102] 1 Cor. 7.

and educate children in fear of the Lord. Thirdly, it establishes such a strong bond between husband and wife that it is impossible for it to be broken in any manner, just as it is impossible to break the bond between Christ and the Church. For that reason, it follows that no man can dispense this law so that a husband might leave his first wife and marry another; likewise that a woman leave behind her first husband and marry another man.

S. *What is required to constitute a Marriage?*

T. There are three things necessary. The first is that both persons should have a suitable capacity for union; *e.g.* that they have attained the legitimate age, and do not have any relation to one another within the fourth degree, or that they have not made a solemn vow of chastity, and like things. The second is that they should furnish witnesses to the Matrimonial contract and namely the proper parish priest or the pastor with care of souls. The Third is that the consent of each party must be free; they must not be compelled by grave fear whether it is expressed in words, or a similar sign. Therefore, it must be held that if one from these three are lacking, the Marriage cannot be valid.

S. *Which is better, to enter into Marriage or preserve virginity?*

T. St. Paul explains this question, when he wrote, "He who joins a virgin in matrimony, does well, but he who does not does better,"[103] namely, by preserving virginity. And the reason is because Marriage is a human affair, but virginity angelic.[104] Marriage is according to nature and virginity is above nature; not only virginity but even widowhood is more excellent than Marriage. For this reason, the Savior said in a certain parable that the seed which fell in good soil now bears fruit thirty-fold, another sixty, and another a hundred;[105] the Holy Doctors so explain that the thirty-fold is Marriage, the sixty-fold is widowhood, and lastly the hundred-fold is virginity.

---

[103] 1 Cor. 7.
[104] Ambrose, De Virginitate, lib. 1.1.
[105] Matthew 13.

CHAPTER X
On the Virtues in General

STUDENT. *Now that the four principal parts of Christian doctrine have been explained, I would like to know what still remains to be learned?*

TEACHER. The parts I have explained so far are those that everyone must know. Just the same, there are certain other things necessary to know, that particularly lead to our end, eternal beatitude, which we strive to obtain; just as there are virtues and vices, so likewise, there are good works and sins. Although we passed over these in silence while I explained the Apostle's Creed and the Ten Commandments, nevertheless I have decided to treat distinctly and in particular on those expedient matters.

S. *Then tell me, what is a Virtue?*

T. A virtue is a quality which is received in the soul and causes a good habit. Just as knowledge makes a good Philosopher, and the art itself makes one worthy of the title of an artificer, so virtue causes a good man to go out and do good works with ease, eagerness, and perfection. But on the other hand, someone that does not have virtue, even if they sometimes do a good work they still do it only with great difficulty and imperfection. I will show this by a comparison. Virtue is similar to an art and its use. Someone seems to you to be an expert in a skill like striking a lyre or a lute. He plays very elegantly and with great facility, even if he doesn't see the strings; but where someone else comes up that is ignorant of the use, indeed he will be able to strike the lyre and rouse out some noise, but still he does not do this expediently or well. So it is with a man that has virtue, e.g. temperance, with great joy and ease he will perform a good work, and by waiting for the suitable and perfect hour, he will fast and not permit food except that it is but once a day. Yet, for one who does not have this virtue, or on the contrary is gluttonous, fasting will be as bitter to him as death, and although he might fast, nevertheless he cannot wait until it is time for lunch. Then at dinner, when he must eat only one meal, he will prepare a small snack which differs little from a dinner.

S. *How many Virtues are there?*

T. While there are certainly numerous virtues, nevertheless the more principal ones to which all the rest are reduced are seven. These are the three Theological Virtues of *Faith, Hope and Charity*,[106] and the four Cardinal Virtues of *Prudence, Justice, Fortitude and Temperance*.[107] There are as many gifts of the Holy Spirit,[108] followed by the Evangelical beatitudes,[109] embracing every perfection of Christian life. There are also seven corporal Works of Mercy,[110] and as many spiritual Works of Mercy about which I will hand down a succinct doctrine.

---

[106] 1 Corinthians 13.

[107] *Wisdom 8.*

[108] Isaiah 11.

[109] Matthew 5.

[110] Matthew 25.

CHAPTER XI
On the Theological Virtues in General

STUDENT. *What is Faith?*

TEACHER. Faith is the first of the Theological virtues regarding God. It is His proper office to enlighten the intellect, rouse it to every belief which God reveals to us through His Church, even if it might be very difficult and more sublime than natural reason.

S. *What is the reason why we are so firmly held to believe a matter of faith?*

T. It is this: Faith rests upon infallible truth, because the whole thing which faith proposes was revealed by God, and God is truth itself, for which reason it is impossible that what God said would be false. This is why, although a man might conclude that faith seems like something contrary to reason (e.g. that a Virgin gave birth), human reason is weak and for that reason it is easily deceived, while God cannot deceive nor be deceived.

S. Therefore, what must be believed with the virtue of faith?

T. In the first place, it is necessary to clearly believe all the articles of the Creed, which we explained above, and especially those articles of faith that the Church established a feast day for in the liturgical year, namely the Incarnation of the Lord, His Birth, Passion, and Resurrection, Ascension, Sending of the Holy Spirit, and the Most Holy Trinity. Next, a man must be prepared to believe everything that Holy Mother the Church shall declare must be believed. Then, he must take care to avoid those things which are signs of infidels, e.g. having the garments of Turks or Jews, to avoid eating meat on Friday (which the heretics do) and like things, because it is not only necessary to profess the faith in heart and word, but even nobly in outward deeds, as well as to show that he has no share in all the sects opposed to the Holy Church.

S. *What is Hope?*

T. Hope is the second Theological Virtue, and is so called because it is borne towards God. Just as we believe in God through faith, so we also hope in God through Hope.

S. *What is the function of hope?*

On the Theological Virtues

T. It is to raise and excite our will to hope in eternal happiness. Also, because this good is so sublime that it would be impossible to aspire to it by the human virtues, it is that supernatural virtue bestowed upon us by God so that we will trust that we will soon obtain that good.

S. *What is this Hope founded on and sustained?*

T. It is founded on the infinite goodness and mercy of God and sustained by it. There is a very certain argument for this, namely that He gave His own Son, and through Him He adopted us as sons and promised the inheritance of the kingdom of heaven, so long as we would do works in conformity to the dignity we received, and He would at the same time allot the grace and assistance sufficient to furnish such works.

S. *What is Charity?*

T. It is the third Theological Virtue which is borne towards God, because through it our soul is impelled to love God above all things, not only as the Creator and Author of natural goods, but even as the One that gives grace and glory which are supernatural goods.

S. *I would like to know whether charity is borne towards creatures as well?*

T. Charity is properly borne to all men and all those things that God made, but with this distinction, that God is loved for His own sake, seeing that He is the infinite good, while all other things are loved for God's sake. In particular, one ought to love his neighbor insofar as he is made in God's image just as we are. For this reason, we take up the word "neighbor" not only in regard to our parents and friends, but to any man you like, even if they are our enemies because each is the image of God and ought to be loved from this motive.

S. *Isn't Charity a great virtue?*

T. It is greater than all others, and so good that if someone had it, he could not lose his salvation so long as he does not lose charity first, since one who does not have it cannot be saved in any way, even if he would possess all other virtues and gifts of God.

CHAPTER XII
On the Cardinal Virtues

STUDENT. *What is Prudence?*

TEACHER. It is the first of the four Cardinal Virtues, which are given such a name because they are the four principal virtues, just as sources of all other moral and human virtues. For, Prudence governs the understanding, justice, the will, the temperance of the concupiscible appetites and fortitude for the irascible appetites.

S. *What is the function of Prudence?*

T. It is to show in every action the due end, suitable means and all the circumstances (such as time, place, manner and like things,) that should be done well in and through all things. For that reason it is called the mistress of the rest of the virtues, and by its nature is considered like the eyes in the body, or the salt in food, or the sun in regard to the world.

S. *What are the vices contrary to Prudence?*

T. Virtue always consists in the mean, and therefore it has two contrary vices which are its extremes. One of the contrary vices of prudence is imprudence, that is the lack of consideration and rashness, and it is found in those who do not consider what they do, whereby they do not regard the true end of their actions nor do they grasp the true means. The second vice is cunning, or carnal prudence, and it is of those who judge the end with great industry and just the same, consider their own advantage in all things to obtain a worldly good. This is why they try to subtly deceive their neighbor and carry out what is pleasing to them in everything. Nevertheless, in the end such men will appear to have been very imprudent because they threw away their supreme good on account of love of a lesser good.

S. *What is justice and what is its function?*

T. Justice is the virtue giving to each what is his own. Therefore, its function is to regard what is equitable as well as just, and apply uniformity in all human dealings, which, at any rate, is the foundation of all rest and peace. If everyone would live contented with himself, and not desire what is someone else's, there would be no more war and discord.

On the Cardinal Virtues

S. *What are the vices contrary to justice?*

T. There are two, one is injustice, which is when someone takes what is another's, or wishes to give less than what he ought in contracts, or even to receive more than what is due to him. The second is excessive justice, when someone is too rigorous and wants to judge everything very strictly according to the rule of justice against the prescription of reason, because in many cases justice must be mixed with mercy. This may be seen in the example of the poor man who, if he could not pay his debt without forthwith suffering the greatest loss, then it will be reasonable and just to forgive him for some period of time to pay it. If one would not do this, he sins by excessive rigor.

S. *What is fortitude and what is its function?*

T. Fortitude is the virtue which makes a man eager to conquer all of the difficulties that impede good work, nay more even extend themselves to the suffering of death, when either the glory of God demands it or certainly we refuse to fail in what we owe. All the Martyrs triumphed over their persecutors by the benefit of this virtue, and likewise all strong soldiers prove they fought bravely in war and related great glory through this virtue.

S. *What are the vices contrary to fortitude?*

T. There are two, fear and rashness. Fear causes a man to easily lose heart, which, at any rate, is borne from a small measure of fortitude. On the other hand, rashness causes a man to throw himself into the most threatening dangers when it is not necessary. Such can be called excessive fortitude (so to speak), and it is not worthy of praise, but scorn because it is not a virtue but a vice.

S. *What is temperance and what is its function?*

T. Temperance is the virtue that places a restraint upon sensual delights and sees to it that a man uses desires of this sort according to the prescription of reason.

S. *What are the vices contrary to temperance?*

T. There are two, namely intemperance and senselessness. Intemperance is when someone gives himself over to excessive delights, and consequently, is excessive in food, drink and like things, which are harmful to soul and body.

Senselessness is when someone proceeds to the other extreme and so flees all delights that he even refuses to preserve his health with necessary foods lest he would feel the slightest delight that food naturally and suitably provides. Nevertheless among men the vice of intemperance is far more common than senselessness, which is why all the saints exhort us to fasting and mortification of the flesh.

CHAPTER XIII
On the Seven Gifts of the Holy Spirit

STUDENT. *What are the Gifts of the Holy Spirit?*

TEACHER. They are the ones that the Prophet Isaiah recalls, namely Wisdom, Understanding, Counsel, Fortitude, Knowledge, Piety and Fear of the Lord.

S. *What purpose do these gifts serve?*

T. That through them we might obtain the perfection of the Christian life, because they are considered like the nature of a ladder by which we progress from the state of sin to supreme Holiness by different steps. Still we must notice that the Prophet focuses on a number of steps apart from these because he saw the ladder coming down from heaven, whereas we see the same thing but we arrange it from the lowest steps that we might so climb again and again to climb up to heaven from earth. For this reason we place the first step in Fear of the Lord, where a sinner places himself at the foot when he considers that he is the enemy of Almighty God. The second is Piety, because one who fears the punishments inflicted upon sinners by God

begins to be pious and obey God, and desire to
serve Him as well as to do His will in all things.
The third step is Knowledge, because one who
longs to do the divine will, asks from God that
He would instruct him about His holy precepts
and laws. God causes him to know all things
that are necessary for him, partly by preachers,
partly by books and partly by inspiration. The
fourth step is Fortitude, because one who knows
the will of God and proposes to serve God in all
things finds that the world, the flesh, and the
devil make many objections to him, and so God
gives this gift of fortitude whereby the man
conquers all difficulties. The fifth step is
Counsel, because the devil, when he cannot
conquer a man by his own strength, turns to
frauds and under the pretext of good adorns the
just man with a fall. But God will not desert
him, rather he will impart the gift of counsel to
him whereby he will prevail against all the
deceits of the enemy. The sixth step is
Understanding, because when a man has
already been trained in the active life and
related many victories over the demon, God
draws and impels him to the contemplative life
and sees to it through this gift of understanding
that he would understand and penetrate the
divine mysteries. The seventh step is Wisdom,
which is the complement of perfection because

he is wise who recognizes the first cause and weighs and orders all his actions to it; but that man, who does not add perfect charity to the gift of understanding, cannot do it. Accordingly, he acknowledges the first cause with the intellect and orders and disposes all things to his final end by charity. Then, because Wisdom joins the affect to the intellect, then it is called wisdom, that is, knowing knowledge, as St. Bernard taught.

CHAPTER XIV
On the Eight Beatitudes

STUDENT. *What are these eight Beatitudes that our Savior taught us in the Gospel?*

TEACHER. They are another ladder through which we attain the apex of perfection. They are similar to the ladder that we devised for the gifts of the Holy Spirit, since seven steps are contained in those seven sentences whereby we attain beatitude. The eighth embraces a sign by which we understand whether a man has climbed up that ladder or not.

S. *Briefly explain this ladder to me.*

T. Christ our Lord dislodged impediments to perfection in the first three steps, through which we attain beatitude. These three are ordinarily said to be desires for goods, desire for honor and desire for pleasures. This is why in the first, Christ says, "Blessed are the poor in spirit," that is, those who voluntarily scorn their goods. In the second He says, "Blessed are the meek," those who yield to all and resist none, or that are known, in the face of ignominious things, to remove them from their back. In the third, he says, "blessed are those who mourn," that is those who do not seek the joy and pleasure of the world, but turn away, as much as they do penance and deplore their own sins. Moreover, He teaches the perfection of the active life in the two following steps, to fulfill their obligations in all things that we are obliged in justice and charity. Forthwith, in the fourth step He says, "Blessed are they who hunger and thirst for justice," and in the fifth, "Blessed are the merciful." In the last two, He draws us to the perfection of the contemplative life, and for that reason He says in the sixth, "Blessed are those who are pure in heart, because they will see God," namely in the second life through glory, which they recognize in this life through the grace of contemplation. In the seventh, He says, "Blessed are the peacemakers for they will be called sons of God," *i.e.* they are blessed who join perfect charity to contemplation, and in turn, direct all things to God, and by that universal arrangement the sons of God go out to, the kingdom of the soul, being like their Father, holy and perfect. The eighth sentence does not contain a new step of perfection, as St. Augustine correctly observes, but provides us with a manifest sign from which we can conclude that perfection is suited to man.

Moreover, this is the sign, to suffer unjust persecutions by our own will, just as gold is tried in the furnace, so in the same way, a man will be just and perfect in tribulations.

CHAPTER XV
On the Seven Corporal Works of Mercy and the Seven Spiritual Works of Mercy

STUDENT. *It only remains to explain to me the Works of Mercy, both corporal and spiritual.*

TEACHER. The Seven Corporal Works of Mercy are reviewed in the Holy Gospel: Feed the hungry; Give drink to the thirsty; Clothe the naked; Receive pilgrims in hospitality; Visit the sick, Console the captives;[111] The seventh work is to bury the dead, as St. Tobit and St. Raphael the Archangel taught.[112] Moreover, the spiritual works of mercy are also seven, namely: To teach the unlearned; To rightly counsel those in doubt; To console those who mourn; To correct those in error; To forgive offense; To patiently suffer injuries; and lastly, To pray to God for the living and the dead.

S. *Could some reason be found to excuse someone from the exercise of these works of mercy?*

---

[111] Matthew 25:35.
[112] Tobit 12:12.

T. There are three reasons that could excuse someone. The first is, if he lacked the necessary means. For that reason we do not read in the Gospel that the poor man Lazarus exercised some corporal work of mercy because he was altogether in need of all of them, and thus he was crowned due to his patient suffering. For that reason, the disposition of God is such that the rich obtain salvation by works of mercy while the poor through works of patience. In just the same way, a man is not obliged to teach others or help them with counsel when he altogether lacks the knowledge, prudence and advantage. The Second reason, is that when someone serves God in a higher state than that of the active life, wherein he has no occasion to exercise corporal works of mercy, such as we see in the desert monks, who were shut up in solitude or in their cells, but they contemplated heaven and were obliged to not desert their holy exercise to go out and acquisition what is necessary to expend Works of Mercy. The third, is when someone can find nobody that is especially in need of Mercy, since they are obliged to not succor anyone but those who could be helped by another and do not have anyone who would help them or could confer Mercy to them. Just the same, it is still true that the time of obligation does not await perfect mercy but can be eager to succor in a better way, when it can in all things.

S. *It seems to me that everyone can perform the last Work of Mercy, which is to pray to God for our neighbor.*

T. That is right, for even the desert monks exercised Works of Mercy because they pray to God that He would assist those who are in need with His grace.

CHAPTER XVI
On Vices and Sins in General

STUDENT. *Now it will be the time to teach me what vice and sin are, so that I can flee them, just as you taught me about the acquisition of virtues and good works.*

TEACHER. There is no other sin than the voluntary commission or omission against the law of God; in that there are three things that are required to perpetrate a sin. The first is in some commission or omission, *i.e.* that someone should wish to do something or carry out some work that is forbidden, or to not do something that has been commanded, e.g. to blaspheme is to commit a sin; to not hear Mass is a sin of omission. The Second is that it is required that the commission or the omission must be against the Law of God because the law of God is a general rule to do good, just as the art of sculpture is the rule for the sculptor. As a result, just as the sculptor is not a good wall maker, nor does he raise walls well who does not work by the prescription of that craft; so also someone who does not live well, nor is a good man as he does not follow the Law of God. On the other hand, by "the Law of God" we do not only receive that law which He gave Himself, such as the Ten Commandments, but also that which He proposed through the Popes and other Superiors of the Church, both spiritual and temporal because they are all Ministers of God and they receive their authority from Him. The third is, what is required for that commission or omission to be voluntary because something that a man does without the consent of the will is not a sin; e.g. if someone were to blaspheme while he slept or had not yet attained to the use of reason, or did not know that a particular word was a blasphemy, and in such a case the man would not sin because he lacked the consent of the will.

S. *Well, now I know what a sin is, so tell me what is a vice?*

T. A vice is a bad habit and a bad customary practice to sin, which is acquired the more frequently that one sins. From that it arises that a man of this sort sins more easily and similarly with greater boldness and joy, just as, for example, we say some man is a blasphemer if it is but a trifle to him as he usually blasphemes, and is a trifle from his manner of life; still, it is a sin to blaspheme and he is a blasphemer, so it is a vice in the way we speak about all other evils.

VICES AND SINS IN GENERAL

S. *Is sin a great evil?*

T. It is indeed the greatest that can be found, nay more, that alone is absolutely and intrinsically evil, more hateful to God than any matter. From there, it is gathered that God did not hesitate to destroy and exterminate the most noble thing He had built only to punish sin. If the prince should have some vessel made of the purest silver or gold that was of great price, and he were to discover in it some foul liquid that so displeased him that he would bid the vessel to be broken and sunk in the depths of the sea, certainly you would say the prince seriously hated that liquid. So, God also made two very precious vessels, one from silver, which is man, and the other from gold which is the angels, and because in each He discovered the putrid liquid of sin, therefore, He threw the angels guilty of sin headlong into the depths of hell and perpetual misery, and daily men who die in their sins fall headlong into the same place of perdition. Lastly, on account of sin He once uprooted the world by the flood and drowned all men (except for Noah and his family, as He preserved them due to justice).

215

S. *What kinds of sin are discovered?*

T. There are two kinds of sin, one of which is original sin, the other is called actual sin. And the latter is divided into two parts, namely into mortal and venial.

CHAPTER XVII
On Original Sin

STUDENT. *What is Original Sin?*

TEACHER. Original Sin is that sin which we are born with, because it descends to us from our first parent in succession. For that reason, it must be noted that when God made the first man and woman, who are called Adam and Eve, He bestowed upon them seven gifts. The first was the grace which made them just and friends of God as well as His adopted sons. Secondly, He bestowed upon them great knowledge to know to do good and turn away from evil. Thirdly, He allotted such obedience to them that the flesh would obey the spirit and would not rebel against reason for the sake of illicit desires. Fourthly, He gave the greatest alacrity and facility to do good and turn away from evil, and He prescribed none but that one and easy command. Fifthly, He made them free from every vexation and fear, because the earth itself produced sufficient fruits for the propagation of human life of its own will and unplowed, nor was there anything that could harm man. Sixthly, he made them immortal, so that they could never die if they were not contaminated

217

with sin. Seventhly, He willed after some time to transfer them to the Heaven, to the glorious and eternal life that the angels enjoyed. But the first man and woman were deceived by the devil, and they did not observe that command and so sinned against God that they lost these seven gifts. Moreover, since God had conferred these gifts upon them not only for their own person but their posterity, so when our parents lost them, they not only lost them for themselves but for us. They not only made themselves partakers of sin but also of every misery, in the same way as they were previously partakers of grace and the goods, which they possessed so long as they would not sin. Therefore, original sin is enmity with God and a loss of divine grace, and we are born with this loss. It is from this sin that all ignorance proceeds, just as wicked inclination, the difficulty to do good and the ease to do evil, the punishment and work of providing things necessary for life, as well as fear and the dangers set about us, the certain death of the body and the eternal death of hell if, before the moment of our death, we will not be freed from sin and restored to grace.

S. *Isn't there any remedy against original sin?*

T. I touched upon this earlier, the remedy is the Passion and death of our Lord Jesus Christ. God willed that He would make satisfaction for the sin of Adam, who as God and man would be free from sin, and therefore, infinitely acceptable to God; He would obey a command not terribly easy, such as the command given to Adam was, but by far the most difficult, the ignominious death on the Cross. And this remedy is applied to us by Holy Baptism, as we said above. Although God did not will to restore those seven gifts all at once, nevertheless, He willed to restore the most principal one, which is the grace through which we are constituted just and friends of God, as well as sons of God and heirs of the heavenly kingdom. Moreover, the remaining gifts will be restored to us with the great rest of the next life, if we will have lived well in the present life.

CHAPTER XVIII
On Mortal and Venial Sin

STUDENT. *Would you explain to me what actual sin is, and why one is mortal and the other venial?*

TEACHER. Actual sin is that which we commit by our own will, after we have attained to the use of reason. Such sins as to steal, to murder, perjure, and like things contrary to the divine law. And this sin is mortal when it deprives us of the grace of God, which is the life of the soul, and makes us worthy of eternal death in hell. Then there is venial sin; seeing that it displeases God, it deprives us of His grace, and indeed merits a temporal penalty, but not an eternal one.

S. *How do I know if something is a venial or mortal sin?*

T. It is necessary to observe two rules so that we would know whether it is mortal or venial. The first, is that the sin must be against the charity for God or neighbor. The second, is that it would proceed from the full consent of the will. If the second of these is absent, it will not be a mortal sin, but venial. So, if a sin is said to be against charity, when it is in a grave matter contrary to divine law, then the offense suffices to dissolve the friendship of God. But if it is committed in some light matter, then it does not suffice to dissolve the friendship of God, so it certainly is not against charity, but it is said to be not according to charity. And so the first sin is said to be against the law, because it is against charity which is the end of the law. The second is not said to be against the law, but it is not according to the law, because it is not against charity but still was not done according to charity. Take this as an example: To steal a great sum of money is a mortal sin, because it is against the law of God and is a grave matter, so in everyone's judgment it suffices to dissolve the friendship of God, and thus it is contrary to charity; on the other hand, to steal a quarter, or a penny or a pin, and similar light matters, is not a mortal sin but a venial one, because the matter is light and although it is not according to charity, still it is not against it because it is not such a thing which could reasonably dissolve the friendship of God. For, if sin is against law and is a grave matter, as well as perfectly voluntary, then it is a mortal sin. But if it was not perfectly voluntary, just as if someone were to notice a sudden thought of stealing or killing or blaspheming before a full voluntary consent could happen, it will be merely venial. For that reason, a man must necessarily attend to himself and turn away from an evil thought or desire as soon as possible, before the will could consent to carry it out.

CHAPTER XIX
On the Seven Capital Sins[113]

STUDENT. *Consequently I desire to know if there are certain sins that are more principal than the rest so that I can avoid them with greater care.*

TEACHER. There are some principal ones, because they act like fonts and roots of many others, and they are called capital in Latin, but in common speech deadly, and they are seven in number. Moreover, there are also other principal sins because they are difficult to forgive, and they are called sins against the Holy Spirit, which are six in number. Lastly, there are other principal sins because they are abominable and against all reason, and therefore they cry out to heaven for vengeance, and these are four.

---

[113] *In Latin they are called capital sins, but in English they are called the "Deadly sins." We have maintained the Latin use because it is necessary to the explanation.* –*Translator's note.*

S. *What are the capital sins?*

T. There are seven of these, pride, or as other say, vainglory,[114] avarice, lust, envy, gluttony, wrath and sloth.

S. *Why are these called capital?*

T. They are not called capital, insofar as they are mortal, since there are many mortal sins, and they are not so called because they are always mortal, for some such as blasphemy, homicide, and several others are not always mortal, while gluttony, wrath and sloth always are. So, they are called capital because they are the heads of many others, which proceed from them like branches from the root and rivers from a font.

S. *What is pride? Do certain sins proceed from it and what is its remedy?*

T. Pride is a sin because a man reckons that he is more than he really is, thus, he wishes to be put ahead of others and cannot suffer one to be higher than him or equal to him. The sins which it produces are to boast of oneself, vainglory, to contend with others, likewise discord,

---

[114] St. Gregory the Great, Mor., lib. 31, c. 17.

disobedience and similar things. Its remedy is that a man will rest upon holy humility with all diligence, *i.e.* that he might understand himself to be nothing, and whatever we have is the gift of God and he should consider others better than himself and hence, esteems himself less than others and subject to all; outwardly and inwardly he will honor men in no matter what degree they are. It also helps to consider in the first place, that pride makes a man similar to the devil, and it is especially hated by God. This is why it is written: "God resists the proud but gives grace to the humble, and confounds those who exalt themselves."[115]

S. *What is avarice? What sins does it give birth to and what is its remedy?*

T. Avarice is a disordered passion for riches and it consists in three things. The first is when a man desires someone else's goods and is not content with his own things. The second is when one desires to have more than what is necessary, nor does he wish, as he is obliged, to bestow what is superfluous upon the poor. The third is when someone posses excessive goods that he loves, even if they are not superfluous such as when someone is not prepared to lose

---

[115] 1 Peter 5.

his goods in a case when it is necessary for the honor of God. For that reason, St. Paul says that avarice is idolatry,[116] because the greedy man puts his goods before God and is more content to lose God than his goods. There are many sins thrust upon us by avarice, such as theft, robbery, fraud in buying and selling, cruelty to the poor and like things. Its remedy lies in the exercise of the virtue of liberality and in the consideration that we are travelers and pilgrims in this life, and for that reason it is especially useful to not burden oneself with these goods but to divide them amongst our fellow pilgrims, that we might carry them together on our journey to our heavenly homeland, and it is more expedient that we prepare to unburden ourselves on our road.

S. *What is lust? What sins does it beget and what is its remedy?*

T. Lust is a disordered passion for carnal desires and delights. The sins proceeding from it are blindness of the mind, rashness, and weakness, as well as adultery, fornication, obscene words and every other sort of uncleanliness. Its remedy is to engage oneself in fasting and prayer as well as to avoid bad company, for

---

[116] Ephesians 5.

these are the means discovered to preserve chastity and apart from these neither to trust too much to one's self nor to his own virtue and sanctity, but to stay very far away from dangers and to guard his senses, by considering the great strength of Samson, the great holiness of David and the great wisdom of Solomon and yet how they were deceived by this vice and incurred a great blindness of the mind, and especially Solomon, who conducted the worship of idols with his concubines.

S. *What is envy? What sins come from it and what is its remedy?*

T. Envy is a sin because the good of another man displeases him since it seems the other man has a greater excellence than he. Here, one must consider that when it displeases someone that another man has a good because he is not worthy or because he abuses it, it is not a sin. Likewise, when it displeases someone to not have the goods which others have, especially virtue, devotion and other goods of this sort, it is also not a sin, nay more, it could even be called holy and praiseworthy. On the other hand, when it seems to someone that to have the goods of someone that obfuscate his glory, and he wants the other man to not have such goods lest he would be equal to him or even superior, then that is the sin of envy. It will also produce many other sins, such as perverse judgment, to have joy when another suffers evil, as well as murmuring, detraction, to seek to diminish the good reputation of one's neighbor due to envy, nay more, he is roused to suddenly commit murder, just as Cain did when he murdered his brother out of envy, and likewise the Jews who prepared the Lord's death from envy. Its remedy is to devote one's self to the exercise of fraternal charity and to carefully weigh envy more to jealousy than to harm by envying. For the envious man inflicts himself and consumes himself inwardly and, God often raises up a thing to be envied in such a way that the envious man who desired the thing is downcast and humbled. We see that the devil repulsed the first man from earthly Paradise by envy, but in the time that God sent Christ into the world, he gave back earthly Paradise due to His merits. The brothers of Joseph the Patriarch sold him through envy, but on that occasion, God saw to it that ultimately he would evade them. King Saul persecuted David from envy, and God took the kingdom from Saul and bestowed it upon David.

S. *What is gluttony? What sins does it beget and what are their remedy?*

T. Gluttony is a disordered appetite for food and drink. Such disorder consists in the eating of more sumptuous food than is suitable, or when someone seeks precious food in excess or eats forbidden foods, such as meat on Friday, or when someone does not observe the appointed hour for eating on a day of fast, or at length, when someone eats greedily and gluttonously. The sins that are begotten from gluttony are the obscurity of the mind, vain joy, and loquaciousness. Often, lust proceeds from gluttony, which then brings in all of its daughters. The remedy is to be vigilant in temperance and abstinence, as well as put the benefit of the soul in a higher regard than that of the body. In particular, one must carefully consider that the delight of gluttony is very brief and very often the pain of the stomach and the head—which follow—are longer.

S. *What is wrath? What sins does it give birth to, and what is the remedy?*

T. Wrath is a disordered desire for vengeance. Nevertheless, it must be noticed that a moderated anger is good and rightly ordered.

231

This is why it is said in the Psalms: "Be angry and do not sin."[117] St. Basil says, "Anger has the nature of a dog, which is good when it is aggressive against enemies but not good when it seeks to bite its friends.[118] The disorder of wrath is in three things. The first is when someone wishes to take vengeance on someone who does not merit castigation, nor has offended him. The second is when someone wishes to take vengeance away from the proper authority, because to avenge and punish an evildoer is only the job of superiors, such as Princes and Magistrates. Since God is the supreme Prince, as a result, He says that He is the one to take vengeance.[119] The third is when someone would set out to take vengeance out of hatred, but not out of zeal for justice in a manner that goes beyond all other circumstances. The sins that are borne from disordered anger are contention, injurious words, beatings, unsuitable acts and if a man were to lose his mind, then the disorder of insanity and similar things. Its remedy is to devote oneself to the virtue of mildness and patience, by considering the examples of the saints and of Christ Himself, Who gloriously

---

[117] Psalm 4.

[118] Basil, *in orat. de ira.*

[119] Romans 12.

triumphed over vices of this sort by forbearance and patience. For, it does not happen infrequently among mundane men that they propose to take vengeance very severely on their own enemies.

S. *What is sloth? What sins does it produce and what is its remedy?*

T. Sloth comes from a Greek word (*acedia*) and has the sense of weariness and contempt, and so it is a capital sin when one tires of any good work and is moved by contempt. Moreover, it displeases him that he is obliged to observe the divine precepts and to persevere in the path of the virtues. The sins that sprout forth from sloth are contempt for commands, and because one throws himself into the prey of vice, he despairs of doing good, and as a result they become rancorous against those that strive to avoid sin and take up a good life. The remedy is not to be lazy, but to busy one's self in good books and to consider the great reward to be given which God promised to those who love Him and observe His commandments; likewise, the eternal and intolerable punishment which He has prepared for those who disregard them.

CHAPTER XX
On Sins against the Holy Spirit

STUDENT. *What are the sins against the Holy Spirit, and how many are there?*

TEACHER. There are six, to despair of salvation, the presumption that one will attain eternal salvation without merits, denial of a known truth, to envy the grace given to another, obstinacy in sin, and final impenitence.

S. *Why are they called sins against the Holy Spirit?*

T. Because they are committed from pure malice, particularly the third one, which is most properly a sin against the Holy Spirit, when someone knowing a truth, nevertheless wishes to obstinately uphold and prove that it is not true. Moreover, a sin committed from malice is called a sin against the Holy Spirit because goodness is attributed to Him, and that is contrary to malice. This is in the same way that to sin from ignorance is said to be against the Son, in as much as wisdom is attributed to Him, so also to sin from weakness is said to be against the Father, insofar as power is related to Him.

S. *What then, is the proper effect of these sins?*

T. Certainly that they are not forgiven either in this world or in the next, as our Savior taught in the Gospel;[120] nevertheless that must be so understood in that they are very difficult to forgive, because it is rare and laborious for those guilty of these sins to come to true repentance, just as we say when there is an incurable disease, we do not mean to say that it can be cured by no way, but that it is rarely cured, nay more, ordinarily it is not cured.

---

[120] Matthew 22.

CHAPTER XXI
On Sins Crying to Heaven for Vengeance

STUDENT. *How many sins are there calling out to heaven for vengeance?*

TEACHER. There are four, namely willful murder; A carnal sin against nature usually called Sodomy; Oppression of the poor—especially of orphans and widows; lastly, Defrauding the laborer of his wages.

S. *Why are they said to cry out to heaven?*

T. Insofar as the injustice of those sins is so manifest that one can in no way cooperate with them, or hide them.

CHAPTER XXII
On the Four Last Things

STUDENT. *Moving on, give me a general outline of how to flee sin?*

TEACHER. The wise man says, "Remember your last things, and you will never sin."[121] Four of these last things are: Death; The General Judgment; Hell; and the Glory of Heaven.

S. *Why are they called the four last things?*

T. Because death is the end of life and the end of all things which can come to mind in this world. The General Judgment is the last of all judgments which will be established, appeal from which to another tribunal will not be given. Hell is the last evil that will befall sinners, in which they will remain forever without any relaxation. The Glory of Heaven is the final benefit to be conferred upon the good that will never be lost.

S. *Well then, tell me what the value is in the consideration of the four last things, is it because I*

---

[121] Eccl. 7.

will not sin, as the wise man you quoted says, if I will frequently call these to mind?

T. There are four points to be considered that come to mind about death. The first is that death is very certain; no one can escape it. The second is that the hour of death is uncertain and many die when they least expected it. The third is that through death all things in this world are ended and torn asunder, and at length the vanity of the world is known. The fourth is that at the time of death, every man shall grieve over the evil he committed and the omission of the good he ought to have done. This is why it is a great folly for a man to do those things for which he shall be sorry.

Then there are these points to consider on the last judgment. The first, that this judgment shall need to be established for grave matters, namely the supreme good and the supreme evil. Second, this judgment is carried out by the Supreme Judge, Who knows all things and Whom no man can resist. The third, is that it will be in the presence of the whole world, and no mortal can haul himself away from it. The fourth, there will not even be the least hope of escaping the last sentence and execution of Divine Justice.

Now, the consideration of hell comes to mind, which is wide, long, deep, and boundless. It is wide insofar as it embraces all punishments imaginable; long in as much as all the punishments are eternal; deep because they will be the most painful and in the greatest degree; boundless because the punishments shall be pure, and mixed with no kind of consolation whatever.

Similarly the glory of heaven must be considered to be full and broad, and to contain every good imaginable, even more than we can imagine or desire. We say it is long, because all those goods are eternal; tall, because all those goods adjoin the highest and noblest; boundless because the goods are true and pure, not violated by the mixture of any evil. In addition, this must be noticed, the goods of the world make up nothing in these four considerations, just as on the other hand, the evils of this world are few, short and scanty, and they are always spread over another sort of consolation. For that reason, you can conclude that a man has really lost his mind and senses, who utterly throws away future goods or falls into future evils for love of this life, or fear of a present tribulation.

FINIS

Made in the
USA
Middletown, DE